Gressenhall Farm a

Gressenhall
Farm and Workhouse

A history of the buildings
and the people who lived and worked in them

by Stephen Pope

POPPYLAND
PUBLISHING

First published 2006

ISBN 0 946148 74 0
     978 0 946148 74 5

Published by Poppyland Publishing, Cromer,
NR27 9AN

Picture credits
Norfolk Museums Service: Gressenhall Farm and
Workhouse, pages 13, 34, 35, 38, 51, 54, 58, 65,
68, 69, 72, 73, 75, 78, 80, 81, 82, 83, 87, 88,
89, 91; Norfolk Air Photography Library, page 43
Poppyland Photographs, pages 2, 6, 16, 19, 22,
26, 28, 30, 31, 33, 36, 40, 44, 60, 61, 63, 66,
67, 71, 77, 93

Designed and typeset in 10 on 14pt Trebuchet
by Watermark, Cromer, NR27 9HL

Printed by Printing Services (Norwich) Ltd

Contents

Acknowledgements

Many people have assisted me in the writing of this book, not least by their support and encouragement.

The staff of the Norfolk Record Office in Norwich have been very helpful in providing the records of the Mitford and Launditch Union, from which this account has been primarily made.

At the Gressenhall Farm and Workhouse, I must thank the staff and my colleagues at the museum, in particular Frances Collinson the museum's Collections Officer, for their assistance and encouragement. I also owe a great debt to the volunteers of the Workhouse Trail Guide team, Mike Turner, John Walker, June Ross, Beryl Amis and the late and much missed Kath Armstrong and Jim Parker, who introduced me to the joys of researching this fascinating building and its occupants.

Last but not least, my wife Ann, a fellow Workhouse Trail Guide and colleague, not only undertook a great deal of the research for the book but also spent many hours patiently reading and commenting on the various drafts.

The responsibility for the final content does, however, remain mine alone.

Stephen Pope

One of the original (1777) doors of the House of Industry at Gressenhall

1 Introduction

THE WORKHOUSE, detested and feared, evoked shame in those individuals who were forced to enter its walls. The workhouse is deeply embedded in the folk memory of this country; children were often warned by their parents that if they misbehaved they would be put into the workhouse. But what was life actually like behind those tall, stark, brick walls? This is the story of the workhouse at Gressenhall in Norfolk, from its days as a House of Industry, through its use as a Union workhouse, an old people's home and today as the county's Rural Life Museum.

We have always had the poor with us. In medieval times poor people were looked after by the church and charitable institutions, as well as by their own families. With the dissolution of the monasteries in the 1530s the problem of what to do with the poor became urgent. The Elizabethan Poor Law Acts of 1597 and 1601 gave responsibility for providing relief to the poor of the parish. Parishes were required to appoint an unpaid Overseer of the Poor and levy a compulsory poor rate on occupiers of land and houses, for the relief of the sick, aged and unemployed. Four types of relief were given: almshouses for the aged and infirm, apprenticeships for children, work for the able-bodied and punishment for the work-shy.

In 1662 the Act of Settlement gave powers to the parish to remove any newcomer back to their own parish — the one where they had been born or a parish in which they had gained settlement. The Act was modified in 1795 to allow a person to be removed to their parish of settlement only if they had become chargeable to the parish.

With the Workhouse Test Act of 1722/1723 parishes were encouraged to build poor houses or parish workhouses. These workhouses usually housed a small number of families and were often run by local men contracted by the

SETTLEMENT

A settlement certificate was written by the parish where a pauper or potential pauper was legally settled. The certificate meant that the parish would receive the pauper back (or otherwise indemnify any other parish to which they became chargeable).

The Settlement Act of 1697 allowed strangers (i.e. vagrants, casuals) to enter a parish only if they had a certificate.

Settlement could be gained in a number of ways: by paying rent of £10 or more, by paying poor rates, by serving as a parish officer, by being a bound apprentice, by serving a year in service or being hired as a labourer for one year.

parish at so much per inmate. At Bawdeswell, for example, the master in 1792 was paid 1s 6d a week for each poor person. Conditions within these workhouses could vary enormously. Norfolk seems to have been slow to use the new act as by 1776 only 24 parish workhouses had been built compared with 89 in the neighbouring county of Suffolk.

By the middle of the 18th century the spread of enclosures, the rise in food prices during the French wars and a succession of failed harvests meant that the numbers of poor were rising rapidly, and also meant that poor rates were increasing dramatically. In 1775 the poor rates for England and Wales were just under £2 million, by 1801 the amount had doubled and by 1833 some £8 million was having to be collected. In some areas local Justices of the Peace produced scales of relief according to an applicant's earnings, size of family and the cost of bread. The most famous of these was the Speenhamland scale drawn up by Justices in Berkshire in 1795.

MONEY BEFORE 1971

Farthing ($\frac{1}{4}d$) = one quarter of a penny

Halfpenny ($\frac{1}{2}d$) = half a (pre-decimal) penny

Penny (1d) = two-fifths of a modern penny

Shilling (1s) = twelve pence, or 5p in modern money

Pound (£1) = twenty shillings

Guinea (1 gn, or £1 1s 0d) = twenty-one shillings

To cope with the rapidly rising numbers of poor, parishes in many places began to come together into Incorporations to build larger workhouses or Houses of Industry to house their paupers.

Mid-Norfolk consisted then, as it does today, of mainly agricultural land centred on the market town of East Dereham. The hundred of Launditch lay to the east while the hundred of Mitford was owned by the Diocese of Ely and included the town, altogether an area encompassing some 50 parishes. Few parishes within these two hundreds built their own workhouses

ENCLOSURE

In the medieval period farming was mainly by the open field system, in which three to five large fields surrounding a village were subdivided into strips, each farmed by a tenant on a strict rotation. Animals were grazed on large areas of common or heath land.

By the 18th century landowners were increasingly attempting to improve their farms by consolidating fields into smaller units and improving the soil by manuring and draining. The commons were divided according to the various grazing rights that went with them. The enclosures were overseen by commissioners appointed by Parliament.

The enclosure of the commons meant that the ordinary labourer lost the right to graze a few animals and was forced to work for wages on the new enclosed farms. The loss of these grazing rights reduced many labourers to destitution and they had to move away to obtain work.

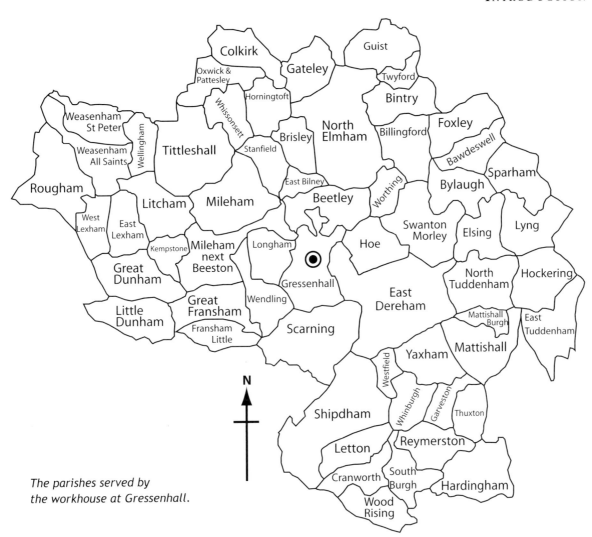

The parishes served by the workhouse at Gressenhall.

The George Inn, Dereham, site of early meetings to set up the House of Industry at Gressenhall.

before 1776, although one was erected in East Dereham in 1758.

On 19th October 1774 a meeting was held at the George Inn in East Dereham to consider presenting an application to Parliament for a bill entitled 'An Act for the Better Relief and Employment of the Poor within the Hundreds of Mitford and Launditch in the County of Norfolk'. The Act would allow the petitioners to build a House of Industry. Houses of Industry were peculiar to East Anglia and were run by a local

HUNDREDS

Shires, or counties, were subdivided into local government units called hundreds. In 1834 their responsibility for poor relief was handed over to the new Poor Law Unions, and the hundreds lost their other functions during the course of the century.

incorporation consisting of directors elected from the hundred. Those attending the meeting included gentlemen, clergy, owners and occupiers of estates in the two hundreds; amongst the signatures were those of the Countess of Leicester, the Earl of Essex, Sir Armine Wodehouse, Lady L'Estrange, Sir Edward Astley and Sir Hanson Berney — all prominent landowners in the county and having estates in the two hundreds. Also present were four local members of Parliament, Wenham Coke, Richard Miller, Richard Jackson and William Clayton. However, the idea of spending all that money out of the rates did not appeal to everyone and the paupers were afraid of losing their traditional ways of getting relief. On the day of the meeting a small mob armed with clubs from the village of Tittleshall attempted to interfere with the meeting but were stopped by local constables who had been positioned at every approach to the inn to prevent just such a disturbance. Throughout October and November the county papers printed claim and counterclaim as to the merits or otherwise of building a House of Industry. One night in November, an incendiary letter was dropped in the yard of James Smyth in East Dereham, one of the proposers for the building of the House. The letter stated that the writer could get 100 people to form a mob to destroy Smyth's and other houses if they persisted in their proposal.

That same month, a very noisy meeting held in the Assembly Rooms at East Dereham rejected the proposal to apply for the act. Many of those attending were small owner-occupiers and tradesmen who could foresee that the building of the house would cause the poor rates to be increased. Many considered that there was no need for a new workhouse since East Dereham already had a sizeable one. This three-storeyed workhouse had been built in 1758 at the bottom of Sandy Lane in the town. During the meeting, which became very noisy, one of the leading proposers, described as a 'noble Lord' (possibly Lord Townshend), stood up and stated that he did not feel bound by the voices at the meeting. Despite all the opposition the bill was presented to Parliament in April 1775 and was granted in May, incorporating some 50 parishes in the area. Within the act was included a penalty of transportation for any damage to the building during its construction.

On 27th June 1775 at the George Hotel, the directors of the Incorporation were appointed. This time the meeting was held outside on the inn's bowling green. Amongst the 59 principal landowners from the two hundreds were Lord Townshend, Sir Armine Wodehouse from Kimberley and Sir Edward Astley from N●●on Hall. Lord Townshend was unanimously elected president; casting of votes for the other directors took six hours. At the end 36 people had been elected as Guardians with another 50 qualifying without election. The directors then turned to the business of electing company officials, Roger Kerrison Esq. becoming treasurer and John Crisp clerk.

Guardians

The terms 'Director' and 'Acting Guardian' were often used interchangeably, though directors seem to have been appointed and were either Justices of the Peace or earned more than £300 a year, whilst guardians seem to have been elected from among people renting property of £100 a year or more.

2 'Pauper Palace'

THE SITE chosen by the directors, or Guardians, for the new House of Industry was Chapel Farm, a 63-acre estate in the parish of Gressenhall some three miles north-west of East Dereham, which was purchased from the Manor of Rougham at a cost of £1,350.

In 1250 Henry III granted to William de Stuteville, lord of the town of Gressendale, seven acres of land in the parish in the area known as Rougham. Here de Stuteville had constructed a college and chapel, dedicated to St Nicholas the Bishop, where a chaplain and his successors would 'pray for his soul, his ancestors and his heirs'. The college was governed by a Master who along with the brethren lived just south of the chapel. During the early part of Henry VIII's reign the chapel was used for parochial purposes. In 1550 it was dissolved and the estate belonging to it was granted to Sir Nicholas L'Estrange by Edward VI, together with considerable lands in nine neighbouring parishes. The chapel building is described in Blomefield's *History of Norfolk* as a 'long narrow building, with a North and South transept and a Chancel'. By the end of the 17th century the building had fallen into disrepair and parts of the chapel are believed to have been converted into a farm house. The precise location of the chapel has never been established, although pieces of stone in the present barn are believed to be from the ruins.

Chapel Farm at the time it was purchased by the Incorporation was owned by a John Rich from Wells next the Sea, up on the north Norfolk coast. The resident tenant was a Tabitha Newman, who received £50 on the termination of her lease on 10 October 1776. Tabitha continued to pay a rent of £45 per annum until she left in April 1777. During the remaining six months of her occupation the directors of the new Incorporation were given access to the site to dig the clay and fire the bricks for the new building.

Records do not show who the architect was, although we do know he was paid a fee of 30 guineas. Construction started in the early summer of 1776 and consisted of a brick centre H Block and an L-shaped extension to the east. Another L-shaped extension to the west was planned but never built as the directors were unable to raise the money. The building was designed to house 600 inmates. Placed on a hill to allow maximum throughput of fresh air for the inmates, it was erected in 15 months. We do not know who the builders were; perhaps many of the labourers would have become the first inmates once the work was completed.

The original part of the House of Industry, built in 1777.

The building was opened on 7th July 1777 but work was still being undertaken in October when it was visited by Lord and Lady Townshend. The report of their visit in the *Norfolk Chronicle* said that 'the sick were well attended and relieved, the aged and infirm comfortably supported and the children instructed in religion and trained to industry' and 'the paupers in general decently and warmly clothed, and also furnished with every necessity of life'. The reporter also enthused that the building, once completed, would 'be the noblest and most beneficial of its kind in the kingdom'. What the directors of the new house thought about this is not recorded but they would probably have been very pleased. The scale of the Houses of Industry built in East Anglia led to them gaining the nickname 'Pauper Palaces'.

The first master and matron were James W. Moore and his wife Margaret. James had formerly been the landlord of the George Inn in East Dereham, the place where the initial

COSTS OF BUILDING THE GRESSENHALL HOUSE OF INDUSTRY

	£	s	d
Act of Parliament	1,060	6	11
Purchase of land	1,422	18	2
Levelling	282	19	6
Building	10,121	6	7
Furniture	1,652	6	0
Farming stock	199	9	11
Solicitor's bill, interest etc.	865	13	11
Printer's bill	41	9	10
	15,646	10	10
Windmill built 1781	207	10	8
Stables and shops added 1786	395	18	4
Total Cost	**£16,249**	**19**	**10**

meetings to set up the House of Industry had been held. Margaret died in 1781 and was buried in East Dereham churchyard. The inscription on her headstone reads:

Here lies Margaret the beloved wife of James Moore of the House of Industry for the MITFORD and LAUNDITCH Hundred, the first and very respectable matron to God pious to her husband faithful to her children affectionate to all benevolent. By her great and unremitted attention to the poor, especially the sick, was seized of a fever of which much lamented by all particularly her husband and family she died July 10th 1781 — Aged 46 years.

That same year James Woodforde, the celebrated parson from Weston Longville, recorded in his diary:

We dined at 3 o'clock and after we had smoked a Pipe etc., we took a ride to the House of Industry about 2 miles West of Dereham, and a very large building at present tho' there wants another Wing. About 380 Poor in it now, but they don't look either healthy or cheerful, a great Number die there, 27 have died since Christmas last.

In 1788 Edward Parry wrote a report for the Society for the Bettering the Condition and Increasing the Comforts of the Poor, which gives a good description of life in the House of Industry and the attitude of the ruling classes towards the building and its inmates. Parry had himself been one of the directors at Gressenhall for some 13 years. The average number of inmates was just under 500 with approximately half being children under 14. These children were often placed in service with local farmers or tradesmen for a year at a time. Parry considered the other inmates to consist of 'profligate men who through idleness and debauchery' had 'reduced their families to depend on the establishment for their support'. He also thought that children should never be put into the workhouse as they became too delicate and unfit for the husbandry labour required in an agricultural district.

Another person to write about Gressenhall during its days as a House of Industry was Sir Frederick Eden. In 1797 he wrote *The State of the Poor*, an investigation into the labouring classes in Britain, which included a chapter on the House of Industry at Gressenhall. At the time there were 539 inmates in the house with 100 of these being illegitimate children. The house was run by a governor and matron, whose salaries were £60 and £25 a year respectively; amongst their duties they were to read prayers every morning and evening, on Sundays to read out the names of the inmates and to ensure the doors of the house were opened at six o'clock in the morning and locked at eight o'clock in the evening in summer or six o'clock in winter. They also had to ensure that all inmates were in their beds by nine o'clock in summer and eight o'clock in winter. Inmates were allowed half an hour for breakfast at eight o'clock, one and half hours for dinner at twelve o'clock and supper was served after they had finished work for the day.

A chaplain was required to conduct services on Sunday, as well as to instruct the children in their catechism and to visit the sick. A surgeon attended daily, medicines being distributed from an apothecary's shop in the building. In 1793 the surgeon was a Mr Webster, who was paid a salary of £63. One Tuesday every month, five Guardians visited the House to inspect the state of the building and the governor's accounts.

Inmate families and old people were housed as family units in rooms known as 'cottages' along the east and south corridor behind an arcade. These cottages were separate rooms each with its own fireplace, and housed married persons, widows or widowers, together with their children. The other inmates were accommodated in separate dormitories on the upper floors with boys and girls in separate lodging rooms of 20 beds, generally sleeping three to a bed. Meals were eaten communally in the dining room which also on Sundays doubled as the chapel. It was found impossible to keep the building clear of vermin due to the constant comings and goings of the paupers.

The men worked on the farm and the gardens, providing much of the food for the house. Hemp was grown on the farm for the making of rope; manufacture of sacks was undertaken in a factory in the main building. This sack factory consisted of looms for weaving the sacks, hemp dressing tools, at least six spinning wheels, a large spinning wheel of six foot diameter and three chain wheels and could produce up to 13,000 sacks annually. The men were also employed to comb wool, dress flax and hemp and weave cloth, the latter being mainly used for the house. A few also worked on the local public roads. The women worked in the kitchen and laundry, as well as alongside the children in the sack factory spinning and sack-making. The spinning produced worsted cloth for manufacturers in Norwich. One of the few surviving documents from the House of Industry days is the spinning records of the inmates, mainly children and women, and the payments they received. The men were allowed 1*d* out of every shilling they earned, while the young women were allowed 2*d* and women aged 60 and above were allowed 4*d*. For making 31 sacks one woman received 10¼*d*. The old men in the House also cultivated a six- to seven-acre garden producing vegetables for the inmates, although no one over 60 was obliged to work. Children were instructed in reading and learning their catechism and were allowed to play outside, weather permitting. At the age of five they were employed in spinning. Girls were also instructed in cooking, housewifery, scouring and washing.

Chapel Farm at this time consisted of some 50 acres and was managed by the governor. On the farm were a dairy and some oxen and sheep. Eight to ten cows were kept to supply the house with milk, butter and cheese. Also down on the farm was a hospital or isolation ward for sick inmates. The Guardians continued to farm the land directly using labour from the house until 1825, when a shortage of able-bodied men forced them to lease out the farm. An advertisement in the *Norfolk Chronicle* on 17th September 1825 gives an indication of the contents of the farm at the time. Up for auction were '4 horses, 3 cows, 9 pigs, 1 road waggon, 2 tumbrils, 2 luggage carts, a horse roll, 2 prs. of harrows, 2 ploughs, cart and plough harness'. Also at the same time some of the machinery from the sack factory was also sold: 'a carding engine, a 30 spindle jack, a blanket loom, a double loom and 2 linen looms'.

Also situated on the west of the main building was a windmill, built in 1781. Once a year the governor purchased a year's supply of wheat

◀ *This book records payments for spinning in 1798*

from the local markets. This was then ground into meal using the windmill. William Pulling from Shipdham was the miller and baker in 1783, being paid *6d* a week. A miller and baker were employed up to 1819 but by 1829 just a baker was employed, which suggests the mill was no longer in operation and its remains were removed in 1837. Also in the main building near the kitchens were a brewery and bakehouse. An area to the west of the building was set aside by the Board in April 1785 for use as a burial ground for inmates.

Sir Frederick Eden's report also details the bye-laws and rules of the House at the time. Any person requiring relief was first to approach their local churchwarden or Overseer, who would attend with the pauper on a Tuesday at the House. Paupers would not be placed into wards until they had been examined by the surgeon, washed and their clothes either cleaned or replaced by new ones. On discharge paupers would be given back their old clothes. Inmates were not allowed to refuse work. Punishment took the form of a reduction in diet, distinction in dress, being placed in stocks or being put on bread and water for up to 24 hours. More serious offences saw the inmate being sent to the local House of Correction at Walsingham. One interesting punishment was reserved for paupers convicted of lying; they were to be 'set in stools in the most public place of the dining room and to have a paper fixed on their breasts with these words written thereon "INFAMOUS LIAR"'.

ROTATION OF DIET IN THE HOUSE OF INDUSTRY, 1797

	Breakfast	Dinner	Supper
Sunday	Milk broth, or onion gruel	Boiled meat, dumplings vegetables and beer	Bread and cheese or treacle, and beer
Monday	Bread, cheese and beer	Pease pottage, boiled in meat broth and milk broth	Bread and cheese or butter, and beer
Tuesday	Onion or plain gruel	As Sunday	Broth and bread
Wednesday	Bread and cheese or treacle and beer	Frumenty; or thick milk with bread	Bread and cheese or butter, and beer
Thursday	Bread and cheese or butter, with beer	Baked suet puddings and beer	Bread and cheese or treacle
Friday	As Tuesday	As Tuesday	As Tuesday
Saturday	Bread and cheese or treacle, and beer	Milk pottage; or onion gruel	Bread and cheese, some butter or treacle and beer

Cabbages, carrots, turnips, potatoes, beans etc. were also served in great plenty during the season.

(Source: Sir Frederick Eden's report)

The diet given to the inmates was relatively generous, certainly compared to that later given in the Union workhouse.

The House of Industry, despite the best intentions of the directors, was never entirely self-supporting. In the main this was due to the inmates largely being elderly or families with

Dietary for the new Union Workhouse, 1836, showing the menu and portions for each day of the week.

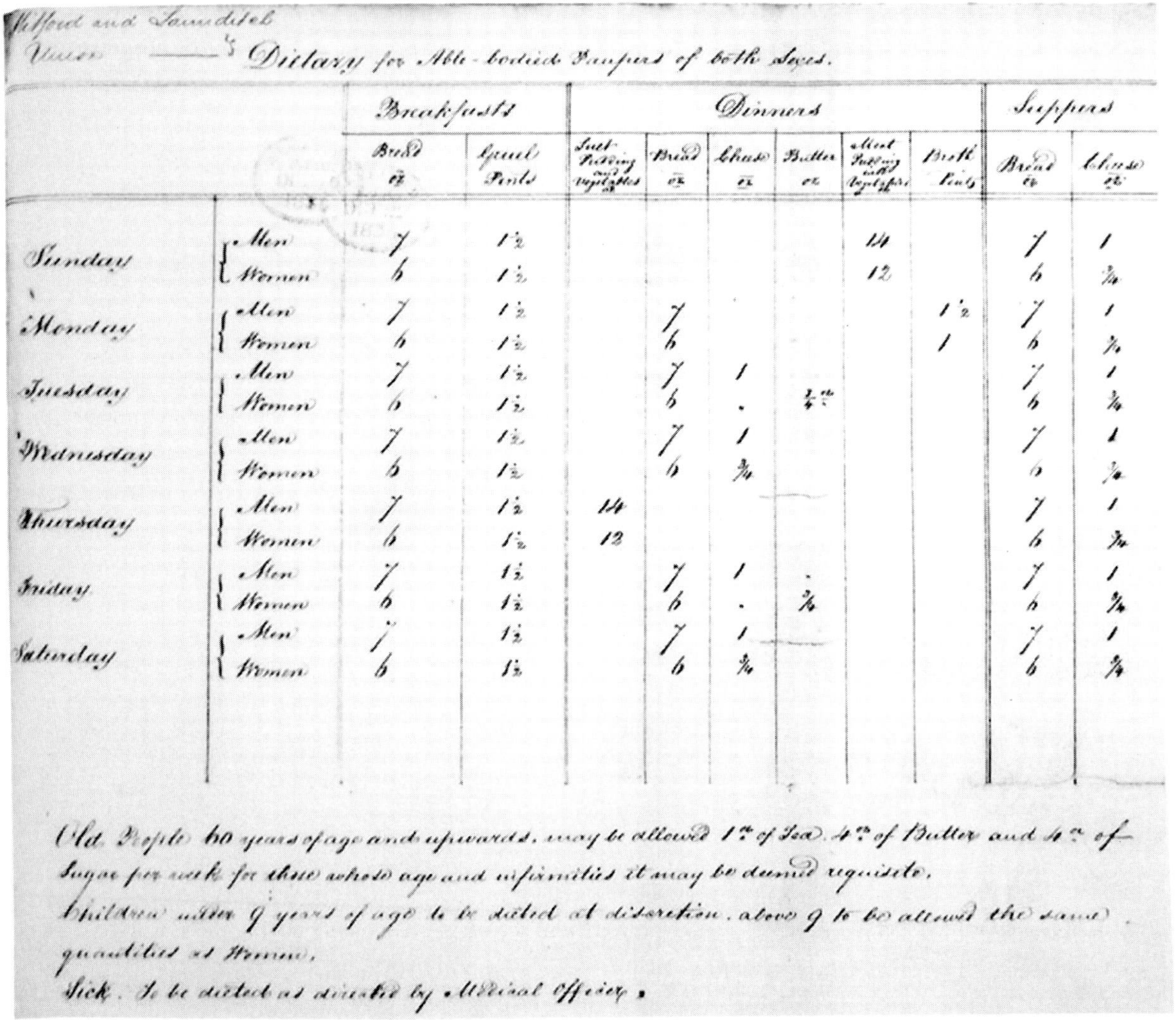

		Breakfasts		Dinners						Suppers	
		Bread oz	Gruel Pints	Suet Pudding and vegetables	Bread oz	Cheese oz	Butter oz	Meat Pudding with vegetables	Broth Pints	Bread oz	Cheese oz
Sunday	Men	7	1½					14		7	1
	Women	6	1½					12		6	¾
Monday	Men	7	1½		7				1½	7	1
	Women	6	1½		6				1	6	¾
Tuesday	Men	7	1½		7	1				7	1
	Women	6	1½		6	.	½			6	¾
Wednesday	Men	7	1½		7	1				7	1
	Women	6	1½		6	¾				6	¾
Thursday	Men	7	1½	14						7	1
	Women	6	1½	12						6	¾
Friday	Men	7	1½		7	1	.			7	1
	Women	6	1½		6	.	½			6	¾
Saturday	Men	7	1½		7	1				7	1
	Women	6	1½		6	¾				6	¾

Old People 60 years of age and upwards, may be allowed 1 oz of Tea, 4 oz of Butter and 4 oz of Sugar per week for those whose age and infirmities it may be deemed requisite.

Children under 9 years of age to be dieted at discretion, above 9 to be allowed the same quantities as Women.

Sick, to be dieted as directed by Medical Officer.

babies. There was also a conflict with local businesses who did not want the House undercutting their own prices. By 1792 the building was housing an average of 436 paupers and was paid for by an annual revenue from the rates of £3,965 18s 1d. This was inadequate to clear any of the outstanding debt, and in the previous year the Treasurer had had to advance £1,000 to the Corporation. To help in this the Guardians applied to Parliament to increase the rates but by 1808 they still had a debt of just under £10,000 outstanding, and most of this had still not been repaid by the time the building was converted in 1836 to the Union workhouse. In contrast the House of Industry built at Heckingham, in south Norfolk, in 1764 had paid off its loan of £7,000 by 1792.

The people of East Dereham had never liked the idea that their own workhouse had been closed and their inmates removed to Gressenhall. In 1801 East Dereham left the Incorporation and their 117 inmates were transferred to a new workhouse built on a ten-acre site at Union Drift on the Norwich Road leading out of the town. Just before they left, the number of inmates in Gressenhall had reached 670, the highest total throughout the building's existence.

WORKHOUSE TEST ACT 1723

Often called Knatchbull's Act after its sponsor, Sir Edward Knatchbull, this Act gave parish officers the power to establish a workhouse and to refuse relief to those who would not enter it.

During the early years of the 19th century the problems of providing for the poor remained and by 1820 poor rates were accounting for one fifth of national expenditure. In 1830 the countryside saw the 'Swing Riots' when gangs of agricultural labourers went around the countryside burning ricks and breaking threshing machines. At this time a third of Norfolk's parishes were in Incorporations or Gilbert Act Unions. The Gilbert Act of 1782 had given powers to local magistrates to sanction new combinations of parishes to build Houses of Industry. In February 1832 a Royal Commission was set up 'For Enquiry into the Administration and Practical Operation of the Poor Law'. Assistant Commissioners toured the country gathering evidence, much of it from East Anglia with its Houses of Industry. The report, written in the main by Nassau Senior and Edwin Chadwick, was delivered in March 1834 and gave rise to the Poor Law Amendment Act in August.

GILBERT'S ACT 1782

This Act provided for a group of parishes to set up a common workhouse to which only the aged and infirm were to be admitted. The able-bodied were to be found work or to be subsidised from the poor rates. The grouping of parishes was meant to reduce the cost of running a workhouse. Before this act, parishes had to go through the burdensome procedure of obtaining a private Act of Parliament to set up an Incorporation.

3 'The Infamous Act'

THE INTRODUCTION of the Poor Law Amendment Act in 1834 had major implications for the relief of the poor. Now there was to be a national system of poor relief under the central authority of the Poor Law Commission. Parishes were to join together in Unions and build workhouses for the poor; these workhouses were to be operated under a central administration and the old parish workhouses were to be abolished and Boards of Guardians elected. The man charged with introducing the new Act in East Anglia was Dr James Kay, Assistant Commissioner for East Anglia between 1835 and 1838. Kay seems to have based his formation of the new Unions on the locations of existing Houses of Industry and Gilbert Union workhouses throughout Norfolk and Suffolk.

Outdoor relief for able-bodied labourers and their dependants was abolished and recipients could now obtain relief only by entering well regulated workhouses. Conditions in these workhouses were to be made 'less eligible' than the conditions of the lowest paid worker outside. The object of 'less eligibility' was to make the workhouse act as deterrent and to serve as a 'self acting test' for applicants seeking relief. Only the really needy would seek to enter the workhouse, the merely idle would be deterred.

The original Mitford and Launditch Incorporation was dissolved in 1836 and the new Mitford and Launditch Union formed. The Union was divided into five districts – Litcham, Elmham, Fransham, Shipdham and Hockering – each with its own Relieving Officer. Later these districts were to form the basis of the registration districts when civil registration was introduced in 1837. The new Union encompassed the original 50 parishes from the Mitford and Launditch hundreds together with another ten parishes transferred from the Eynesford hundred. With the introduction of the Union the parish workhouses including the one at East Dereham were closed and their inmates transferred to Gressenhall.

Substantial alterations were made at Gressenhall to accommodate the requirements of the new act. Included amongst these was the removal of the 'cottages' in which the pauper families had lived under the old Incorporation, the blocking up of the arcades on the ground floor and the construction of dormitories and day rooms. Around the site a wall was erected to enclose the building and the work yards. The wall gave the building the look of a prison, and it is not surprising that the poor people gave the new Union workhouses the nickname of 'Bastilles'.

Starting in May 1836 the conversion work was

The wall in the men's exercise yard. Inset: 19th-century inmates have carved their initials on the wall.

carried out by a Mr Fuller Coker Junior from Shipdham and was completed by September. The cost was £4,358, from which was deducted the £796 cost of the bricks, which are believed to have been made on site, possibly by the inmates. Certainly Mr Coker used inmate labour as £11 was received for the labour of John Wilkins, Henry Baxter, both inmates, and some of the boys in the house. The original plans for the conversion had not provided accommodation for a shoemaker or tailor and room had to be found for these two tradesmen by erecting a false wall in one side of the Women's Receiving Ward. To pay for all the alterations the Guardians were allowed by the Poor Law Board to borrow some £4,800 from Messrs Gurney & Co Bankers in Norwich.

With the building changes finished by September 1836 the inmates were separated into their respective wards, men, women and children. The Guardians were concerned that riots could break out when the inmates were separated, as had happened in another workhouse at Heckingham. At Gressenhall there were police on duty during the period of the move but there is no record of any disturbance. While the new regulations were being implemented the last master of the House of Industry, Edward Tice, was still in post. Whether he agreed with the new regime is not known, but by 1837 the Guardians had appointed George Pinson and his wife Rhoda as the master and matron at a salary of £80 and £20 respectively. Among other staff members appointed to implement the new regime were Robert and Mary Rudd as schoolmaster and schoolmistress and John Everett as porter, to control entry to the building.

A number of former paupers were also given employment in the workhouse. When the Guardians advertised for a nurse at a salary of £7 per annum, the post was filled by Mary Kittle, an inmate. Early nurses in the workhouse were all recruited from among the inmates; with limited nursing skills, they would mainly have been employed to clean and feed the sick. Other staff appointed at the time were William Baxter, an inmate from Hardingham, as messenger, and in the trade of shoemaker Samuel Melton, from Tittleshall, employed at seven shillings a week to make and repair shoes for inmates and to instruct the boys in the school in the craft.

The adjacent Chapel Farm had been let by tender by the Guardians since 1825. At the time of the changes it consisted of 42 acres, 3 roods and 23 perches of arable and pasture land. In September 1836 the tender was awarded to John Burton who paid £44 for half a year's rent on what now became Union Farm. The tender specifically requested that the tenant use the Norfolk four-course rotation for crops. Burton's tenancy ran for four years; the tenancy was then awarded to Samuel Pearce from Holt for 12 years at a rent of £120 per annum. The new tenant soon started improvements on the farm, the Guardians authorising and paying for the erection of cattle sheds on the south side of the barn.

LAND MEASUREMENT

Acre. A unit of area standardised by Edward I at 40 rods by 4 rods. Today it is measured as 4,840 square yards or 0.405 hectares. It is said to be the amount of land a ploughing team (two horses, man and plough) could plough in a day. Strictly speaking it is the distance an ox team ploughed in a day (oxen are slower). In ploughing an acre the ploughman would walk 11 miles.

Rood. One quarter of an acre, 660 feet long or 40 square perches in area.

Rod, pole or **perch.** Linear measure of 5½ yards (16½ feet, or 5.029 metres), or an area of 30¼ square yards.

Rumours as to what went on in the 'new' Union workhouse were soon circulating around the district. During August 1837 persistent reports from the local parishes talked of a child that had died in the workhouse from starvation. The Guardians took these rumours very seriously and instigated a through investigation, finding that there was 'not the least foundation for such a report'. The Guardians did attempt to make life a little better by laying out a series of broad walks on wasteland just outside the entrance gate for use by the aged inmates. They also created gardens for employment of the boys.

During a visit to Gressenhall in 1837, Dr Kay (later Sir James Kay-Shuttleworth), the Assistant Poor Law Commissioner for East Anglia, found the boys' school in the charge of a 13-year-old boy called William Rush. William, who had been top of the little school, had taken charge when Robert Rudd, the schoolmaster, had fallen ill. As observed by Doctor Kay 'the whole discipline and routine of the garden workshop and class instruction went on unbroken'. The chairman of the Guardians, Mr Frederick Walpole Keppel, also observed William in action and immediately authorised him to continue his work. Kay recommend that Rush be regarded as the apprenticed assistant of the schoolmaster, and when Rudd recovered the Guardians employed William as his assistant teacher. Kay had already seen a similar system in operation in Holland and devised the pupil

teacher system where the brightest child from the class was used to teach younger children. However, the pupil teacher system does not seem to have been adopted by many Union workhouses, although it later became a major part of the National Schools. William Rush himself was sent by the Guardians to Mr Aubin's school at Norwood in London to continue his

Two years after visiting Gressenhall, James Kay, then in his thirties, became Secretary to the Privy Council Committee on Education; he helped begin school inspections and founded the first teacher training college in the country, at Battersea.

training. Later he was sent to Battersea Training School and became a fully qualified teacher. By 1849 he was employed as the schoolmaster at West Beckham workhouse in north Norfolk. Later he moved to Broadstairs in Kent but died shortly afterwards from tuberculosis. The 1851 census shows that two other boys from Gressenhall had also become pupil teachers, William Park from Hockering and William Seaman from North Tuddenham.

In July 1838, Robert and Mary Rudd the schoolmaster and schoolmistress were called before the board and given notice they would be dismissed at the end of the present quarter for general misconduct. At the same time, William Baxter, the messenger, was also dismissed. In a letter to the Poor Law Commission it would seem that it was Mary Rudd who was guilty of the offence. What the offence was the Guardians' minutes do not show, but it may concern some sort of affair or misconduct between Mary and William Baxter. Whatever it was, in Victorian times the wife's behaviour was considered the responsibility of the husband and of course both had to be dismissed. William Baxter was luckier; the master, George Pinson, requested the board to reconsider his case and he was reinstated. The following month the board appointed the daughter of the master, Harriet Pinson, as schoolmistress and a John Gibson from Norwich as the schoolmaster. Gibson served until March 1840 before resigning and being replaced by Robert Bradfield from Brisley.

Bradfield was to serve at Gressenhall for the next 34 years.

With so many people living in such close proximity outbreaks of disease were a recurrent fear of the Guardians. In 1834 cholera and scarlet fever had killed one sixth of the inmates in the workhouse and during April 1839 the Guardians began to view with anxiety an increasing rate of sickness, mostly due to some 100 cases of influenza. The board gave the medical officer, Mr Warcup, authority to summon assistance from the other medical officers in the Union should he so require. By May of the following year, Warcup was being required to attend sick paupers at Gressenhall at least twice a week with the other days covered by his assistant, Mr Leek. In August 1844 the children in the workhouse were afflicted by an outbreak of measles and typhus. Two inmates, Mary Ann Nichols and Lucy Loveday, were awarded five shillings each for nursing the children during the outbreak. Other diseases prevalent in the workhouse at the time were scarlet fever, ringworm, whooping cough, chicken pox, phthisis, ophthalmia and consumption. A common complaint was the 'itch' which seems to have been a general term used for any type of skin disease, hence the 'Itch Ward' where paupers were received into the workhouse.

Despite early teething troubles the Guardians seem to have been happy with the administration of the new Act. In March 1841 they sent a letter to the Secretary of State for the Home

Department, Lord John Russell, praising the introduction of the new law, stating that the average annual expenditure on relief for the three years up to April 1835 had been £26,684, while for the six months commencing July 1835 the Guardians had only spent £6,967. Despite the strictures of the new law, outdoor relief to the aged, infirm and sick does seem to have continued, as it did in many rural Unions. However, for the 'idle and profligate' the only relief was the workhouse. The Guardians were also in favour of the regular system of education implemented in the workhouse, the 'natural benefit of a Christian Education' providing a means whereby the children would become 'servants and useful members of Society'.

George Pinson and his wife Rhoda, the master and matron, resigned in 1843 to take up the post of governor of Norwich prison, in the castle. Pinson had been very well thought of by the Guardians, as well as the inmates. He was replaced by George Francis Whelan and his wife Emma in January 1844. Whelan did not seem to get off to a very good start, being posted absent without leave, to the concern of the Guardians who feared that the workhouse was being left without a master in charge. A month later Whelan was again reprimanded by the board for not keeping the books of the Union up to date and for being absent from the House more than he was allowed; he was also accused of making false entries in his Master's Report Book. In June 1845 Whelan again found himself being severely reprimanded by the board for neglecting his duties, this time along with the schoolmaster, Robert Bradfield, for allowing two boys, William Bales and Dennis Blockwell, to escape from the workhouse between four and five in the morning. The boys were able to escape because the doors were not properly locked, a task supposedly undertaken as part of the schoolmaster's duties.

Locking the present gates, made and donated by an international range of craftsmen. When the building was a workhouse, the gates were solid wood, completing the encircling walls.

To assist the Guardians in their work of administering the poor law a clerk had been appointed. The first of these, Samuel King, resigned in June 1844. However, it may have been a case of him jumping before he was pushed, as later that year proceedings were taken out against him for deficiency in his accounts. Charged with embezzling several sums of money, King absconded from Litcham in May 1844 and went to live at Soham in Cambridgeshire. He was still at large in October 1845 when Charles Wright, the new clerk, was asked whether there was any further information on King's whereabouts and whether the Guardians were still contemplating any further proceedings. The clerk was instructed to reply that the Guardians were not. Twenty years later, in 1865, the Solicitors of the Treasury were still investigating the theft of the money.

During the later part of his time at the workhouse, Mr Whelan, the master, had requested that his son John be allowed to stay in the building for a month. The Guardians were a little put out to discover that the boy had in fact been residing in the workhouse for some months previously without their knowledge. By February 1846 Whelan himself seems to have been unwell as the Guardians were becoming concerned that he was unable to attend to his duties, the able bodied men's ward being looked after by his wife Emma, the matron. In June Whelan had still not recovered and he tendered his resignation. Despite his early problems Whelan was highly thought of by the Guardians, who regretted losing his services. During their time at the workhouse the Whelans had found situations for some 40 inmates. They left to take up a post at Haydock Lodge Lunatic Asylum, taking some four inmates from Gressenhall with them into their service at the Asylum.

In 1847 the Poor Law Commission was replaced by the Poor Law Board. Since its formation the Commission had been the target for much criticism and by 1845 it had too little power and too few staff to implement its decisions. The Andover scandal in the same year did not help with its revelations that inmates at the Andover Union workhouse had been starving and fighting amongst themselves for pieces of gristle and marrow on old bones they were breaking for fertilizer. The inmates had been punished by the master and placed on a reduced diet but the scandal was such that the practice of breaking bones in workhouses was soon banned although the practice does not seem to have been carried out at Gressenhall. The Poor Law Commission had been an autonomous body with no representation at government level, but the new Poor Law Board was now responsible to Parliament with its own Minister.

Animals were certainly not allowed into the workhouse, but in October 1847 the Visiting Committee were made aware of a dispute between the master, Stephen Wade, and the schoolmaster, Robert Bradfield. Bradfield had for a number of months been keeping a dog on the premises without the knowledge of the Guardians. The dispute had brought forth 'very improper language and behaviour' between the two men, who were suitably admonished by the chairman, the dog being removed from the workhouse. A later master, Henry Harrison, also was taken to task, this time for keeping chickens in the workhouse, finally being allowed to keep a maximum of ten. Whether any of the eggs found their way to the inmates is unknown.

During the middle of 1849 the Guardians became aware that the medical officers of the Union were prescribing medicines without actually seeing patients. This practice had come to light during the case of Rebecca Buck. Rebecca, from the parish of Weasenham All Saints, had been an inmate of the workhouse having been refused out relief. On 27th July she left the building with her three children and returned to Weasenham. Two days later she applied to the local Overseer for readmittance to Gressenhall, but was refused. The next day she travelled to Longham and applied to the Relieving Officer there, who also refused to give her a ticket. Nothing daunted she travelled onto Gressenhall and presented herself at the gate of the workhouse, but was again refused entry, this time by the master. Walking back into Gressenhall village she obtained a 'casual poor' order from the Overseer. However, this was to no avail as she was still refused admission and she returned to Weasenham. Four days later, complaining of a pain in the stomach, she again applied to the Overseer for a note to see the medical officer and was again refused. On applying directly to Mr Raven, the medical officer at nearby Litcham, she was sent medicine. That evening the pain was worse and the medical officer sent calomel and opium, but still did not visit Rebecca. The next day Rebecca was finally visited, although only by the medical officer's assistant who thought that she 'did not appear to be in any danger'. Despite this, Rebecca died that evening at 8 o'clock of 'inflammation of the stomach and bowels probably brought on by catching cold'. The subsequent investigation determined that the master, Stephen Wade, had no power to refuse admittance if the pauper had a proper order. The medical officers were also cautioned that in the future they were not to prescribe medicine without seeing the patient.

The fist-shaped knocker on the porter's door

4 Life in the Workhouse

HAVING BEEN forced to enter the workhouse, what was life like for inmates during the early years after the implementation of the 1834 Act? What level of destitution had driven them to apply to the parish Relieving Officers in the first place? What were their feelings of dread as these desperate people presented themselves at the big wooden gates at the top of the drive from the road? To gain admittance there was the bell or the great knocker shaped like a fist on the porter's gate, still there today. Control of entry to the site was by the porter, who was on duty all day to receive inmates or visitors. The paupers clutching their orders for admission had to present themselves before 8 o'clock in the evening in summer or 5 o'clock in the winter. By 1840 this had been altered to 5 o'clock in summer and 4 o'clock in winter. On entering the courtyard they were conducted to the Receiving or 'Itch' Ward. Here their clothes were removed; they were given a bath, a medical examination and issued with a set of workhouse clothes. They were then separated into their appropriate wards.

Inmates were classified into seven classes within the workhouse and were not allowed to keep any personal possessions, these being removed on entry and either stored for return to the inmate on leaving or more usually sold, to help defray the cost of their maintenance in the workhouse. Of their clothing, anything that was usable would be cleaned and put into store, although much of it would have been verminous or in a bad state of repair. Items from the store would be issued to inmates on leaving the workhouse to go into service. Uniforms were made from either drill, a coarse twisted cotton or linen fabric, or duffel, a coarse woollen cloth with a thick nap. Women's clothing was usually made of Haverhill drabbett and olive calico with apron checks. For the men there were also blue check handkerchiefs. An advertisement for supplies to the workhouse, placed in the *Norfolk Chronicle* in March 1837, gives an indication of the type of material used for the clothing issued:

Stout Twist Calico, grey and white for shirts, hats, and capes for men and boys. Flannel and serge for women's petticoats. Calico for shifts, Cotton Checks and Blue Calico. Blue Check Handkerchiefs. Haverhill Drabbett. Leather for shoes.

It was the act of separating the families that most of the poor people feared on entering the workhouse. However, families were allowed to meet for one hour on Sunday during the church service and inmates were allowed to receive visitors, between the hours of 9 o'clock and 5 o'clock in summer and 9 o'clock and 4 o'clock in winter. These visitors were probably members of the family who would bring news of jobs in the area and on occasion also managed to smuggle in items for them. In August 1856 Charles Cole 46, from East Dereham, was visited by a Mrs Rust. The next morning he was found dead, apparently under the influence of intoxication. The coroner's inquest gave the verdict 'That the said Charles Cole died by the visitation of God accelerated by partaking too freely of Brandy clandestinely introduced into the Workhouse by Mrs Rust'. Mrs Rust was taken to the magistrates for 'introducing spirituous liquors into the Workhouse'. Charles Cole was buried in the workhouse burial ground on 12th August.

Two other classes were also to be found in the workhouse, tramps (or 'casuals') and 'Jacket Women'. Both these classes were accommodated in separate outbuildings on the site. By the 1840s there was a regular body of nomadic men who frequented the casual wards of the Union workhouses. The majority of them were between 15 and 25 years old and it was estimated that there were some 40,000 to 100,000 of them in England and Wales. These mainly able-bodied men were admitted to the workhouse and put to work such as pumping water for 3½ hours, in return for food and lodging.

The 'Jacket Women' were single mothers with, as the records describe them, 'bastard children'. They were forced to wear a distinctive

INMATE CLASSES

Class 1   Aged and infirm men

Class 2   Able-bodied men above 13
            (raised to 15 in 1842)

Class 3   Boys between 7 and 13

Class 4   Women infirmed though age

Class 5   Able bodied women and girls above 13
            (raised to 16 in 1842)

Class 6   Girls aged 7 to 13

Class 7   Children under 7
            allowed to stay with their mothers

Iron bedsteads as introduced in the 1830s.

jacket to differentiate them from the other, 'respectable', women in the workhouse. They were looked upon as being morally inferior and in some cases had been deliberately placed in the workhouse by their families. A ward specifically for the 'Jacket Women' was constructed in July 1837 by Mr Edward Sussens from North Elmham, at a cost of £70. Sussens does not seem to have done a good job as in the following year the two cottages were in need of repair, it taking until December before he agreed to do the work at his own expense.

Inmates were housed in dormitories of between 20 and 30 people. Before 1836 the beds had been mainly constructed of wood with a straw-filled mattress on top, but by the end of the year many were being replaced by iron bedsteads. The beds were narrow at the foot to allow more of them to be fitted into the room if required. Children could be made to sleep three to a bed whilst even women were sometimes made to sleep two to a bed. For some of the children this probably would have been the first time they actually slept in a bed, for in many poor people's cottages the children would have slept on straw on the floor or on top of a box. The dormitory floors were mainly bare wooden boards, although by 1857 rugs were purchased.

Life in Gressenhall was very regimented, controlled by the bell in the clock tower on the roof above the dining room. The clock is still there today, although it still has problems in

The clock and bell-tower today

keeping time, a fact that concerned the Guardians back in 1841 when Jeremiah Rust lost the contract after being unable to explain to their satisfaction why the 'clocks belonging to the Workhouse do not work with regularity'. During

Original clockwork now on display

the summer inmates were roused from their beds by the sound of the bell at quarter to six; half an hour was allowed for breakfast before they started work in the yards at 7 o'clock. Dinner was taken between noon and one o'clock, after which they were back in the yards for another 5 hours. After supper at six, the inmates were put to bed at 8 o'clock. In winter the only change to this routine was that the inmates did not get up until quarter to seven and only worked for four hours in the morning.

The inmate's day consisted of monotonous work in the work yards surrounded by high walls. Here the able-bodied men were employed in breaking stones, pumping water and carting gravel and manure. Charles Dickens mentions oakum picking in *Oliver Twist*, written in 1837, but it was not until 1854 that the practice was introduced at Gressenhall. One of the inmates, Benjamin Watts, received seven shillings for instructing the able-bodied paupers in the

PICKING OAKUM

Oakum is the loose fibre obtained by picking apart old rope (usually from ships' rigging) and was used as caulking to seal the hulls of wooden ships. The rope for the Gressenhall inmates to pick apart came from dealers in Lowestoft and Great Yarmouth and the finished product when returned to the dockyard seems to have been mainly used to seal the hulls of the many fishing boats from these ports.

workhouse in the technique of picking and packing the oakum. Later that year in November, the Poor Law Board also allowed the Guardians to punish able-bodied women by putting them to work picking oakum. The practice of oakum picking, although introduced into the workhouse to provide repetitive work for the inmates, did provide a small amount of money for the Union. However, the inmates did not take kindly to the new practice and a number were taken before the magistrate for refusing the work. Others, like John Walden from Swanton Morley, were caught trying to deceive the master as to the amount of oakum they had picked, by stealing already picked oakum from the workhouse stores.

The method used to pick the oakum is not clear. In a number of workhouses it was carried out by women and children picking the rope apart with their bare hands. The rope was usually ships' rigging and would have had to be soaked to loosen the fibres. Oakum is sometimes described as 'beaten' and 'unbeaten' which suggests that a mallet may have been used to loosen the fibres. Despite this treatment the children's hands would have suffered great damage as they handled the rough rope. Other possible methods included a bent nail to help prise the fibres loose from the rope, or a metal spike mounted on a leather patch worn on the thigh, on which the rope would be pushed to break it apart. Oakum picking was a favourite work given to tramps and vagrants and the term 'going on the spike' used by the tramps, which seems to have appeared around 1866, meant to enter a workhouse and may refer to the use of a spike to pick oakum. The oakum was kept in

This display at the museum at Gressenhall gives an impression of what picking oakum involved.

a store in the centre of the building, a practice that caused concern to the Guardians in 1857 and resulted in increased insurance premiums. The practice of oakum picking continued at Gressenhall until 1925 when it was finally considered that the associations connected with the task were undesirable. Only two classes of people in this country picked oakum, prisoners in jail and inmates of workhouses. This seems to have been another example of the lowly status of the workhouse inmates, considered as no better than prisoners just because they were poor.

Inmates did not always meekly carry out the tasks they were allotted. In April 1850 a Richard Burch, age 61, from Dereham, wrote to the Poor Law Board complaining that he had been ordered to break stones in the men's yard. The Guardians surprisingly showed leniency towards Burch, and considered that his former social position as an auctioneer/appraiser meant that he was unsuitable for manual labour.

The women worked in the kitchens cooking, and also in the laundry yard washing and cleaning clothes. The women working in the laundry were given an allowance of four pints of beer per week. Women also carried out the domestic cleaning around the wards and the building. Certain women were also involved in treating the sick. No rewards were supposed to be allowed to the inmates, though by the 1840s some inmates were receiving gratuities for work

The laundry yard, photographed in 1974.

done. One such was Honor Dickerson, who received £1 for her services in the laundry.

The Poor Law Amendment Act of 1834 provided for the education of children in the workhouse and children between the ages of 5 and 10 attended school, girls and boys in separate classrooms. The reason behind these children being given a rudimentary education was that the Guardians and the Poor Law Board thought that if the children had an education they were less likely to return to the workhouse in later years as they would be able to get jobs. James Kay, the Assistant Commissioner for East Anglia, was very interested in improving the education of children in workhouses. In 1837 he arranged for a Mr Horn, a teacher from Scotland, to instruct Robert Rudd the workhouse schoolmaster in the new methods being introduced in schools in Scotland. Children were initially taught the four R's (reading, writing, arithmetic and religion) and by 1842 history and geography had

Flower beds at the front of the building, in a photograph thought to date from the early 20th century

also been added to the curriculum. The number of infants in the workhouse meant that by 1850 an Infant schoolmistress was appointed. Outside of the school the children were also required to undertake tasks in the house. The boys were employed in the gardens in front of the main gate and later were also used on the Industrial Farm. They were also allowed to play for two hours in the morning before entering school and two hours in the evening in summer or between 2 o'clock and 4 o'clock in winter, weather permitting. There is no mention of the same privilege being given to the girls. In January 1843 the Guardians authorised the felling of a tree on the farm to enable a swing to be constructed in the children's yard. When they reached the age of 15 the children were removed from the school and placed in the able-bodied wards. However, in 1858 much discussion resulted from a proposal to allow certain older children to remain in the schools, these in the main being handicapped in various ways. When children left the workhouse they were given a Prayer Book and Bible.

The Guardians would also occasionally make exceptions to the rules and allow older children to attend the workhouse schools. In December 1866 Charles Chilvers at the age of 16 was put into the school to 'avoid objectionable inter-

course with the able bodied men'. Charles had been admitted from the village of Rougham some six years earlier having been a patient in Lynn Hospital where his leg had been removed. At the time the Guardians authorised extra diet for the 'preservation of his life', despite his father earning 14 shillings a week as an agricultural labourer. Two years later they paid for an artificial leg.

Detail from the punishment book of 1897

Punishment at the workhouse could be very severe for what today would seem to be trivial offences. 'Refractory conduct' resulted in incarceration in a cell or room in solitary confinement and being fed on bread and water. Honor Dickerson, mentioned above, was confined in the 'Dungeon' for eight hours, for throwing bread over the wall separating the women's and men's yards. Honor left the workhouse in April 1845 and went into the service of George Pinson the former master, now governor at Norwich Castle jail, and was allowed to leave her children behind at Gressenhall, paying £1 5s 0d for their maintenance out of her wages.

For more serious offences, such as assault or damage to workhouse property, the inmate would be sent before the magistrate and if convicted sent to prison. The Guardians also considered the playing of cards and gambling an immoral act perpetuated by the idle poor. In June 1845 when four inmates, George Backlog, William Goole, James Kendle and George Watling, were found playing cards in the building they were all sent before the magistrates. The four were sentenced to 21 days at the House of Correction at Little Walsingham. Both the master, George Whelan, and the porter, John Carey, were also called before the board and reprimanded for allowing such a 'crime' to happen in the workhouse and also causing the inmates to be awarded their punishment. At the same time the tailor, William Gibson, who had

also been aware of the card playing and had not reported it to anyone, was dismissed from the workhouse. How the cards were smuggled in is not known as inmates were supposed to be searched on their arrival at the workhouse and all personal possessions taken away.

Before 1836 the inmates' diet had been relatively generous with meat and vegetables served regularly. After 1836 the meals became monotonous although adequate in quantity. The dietary tables were fixed by the Poor Law Board in London and the Guardians had to get permission from them to make any changes. Meals were eaten in the main dining room where three rows of benches stretched the length of the room. At the head of the hall was another table at which sat the master and his staff. On this table was positioned a pair of scales used to weigh the plate of food should an inmate dare to question whether they were receiving their entitlement. The food was placed on the table; then the inmates, eating in separate sittings, were allowed in, first the men, then the women and lastly the children. Each sitting had to be cleared away before the next so that the classes did not have contact with each other. This practice of putting food on the tables before the inmates entered was not finally abolished until 1944.

The main treat the inmates received was of course Christmas. It was paid for out of the pockets of the Guardians themselves, for the

Poor Law Board in London would not sanction expenditure for such frivolities; the proposal for Christmas dinner went before the board every year. In most cases it was accepted, but in 1856 when it was put to the vote the proposal was defeated and that year no Christmas dinner was given to the inmates. Christmas dinner was not however, given to all in the workhouse. Neither the able-bodied men, usually tramps, nor the Jacket Women were entitled. The *Norwich Mercury* in January 1852 details the food given that year at Christmas:

The inmates of the Mitford and Launditch workhouse, 390, were bountifully supplied with roast beef, plum pudding, ale and tobacco, on Christmas day. The women, in addition, had tea, sugar, butter and snuff; and the juvenile branches had afterwards nuts and oranges given them. The day was altogether to them one of great joy and cheerfulness. They desire to express their grateful thanks to the Guardians for this liberal feast.

At other special times the inmates could also receive extra rations. For example, the Coronation of Queen Victoria meant that they received a pint of ale and beef and plum pudding. On the occasion of her marriage to Prince Albert the old men and women and children under 16 received ale and buns. On a number of occasions on Whit Tuesday the aged and infirmed inmates regularly received a pint of beer.

Inmates could leave the workhouse at any time by giving three hours' notice, but usually had to have a job waiting for them and the whole family had to leave together. Any able-bodied men could be hired out to local farmers. For widowed mothers the Guardians sometimes allowed the children to be left behind, the mother having to pay maintenance out of her wages. For the orphan children, the boys would be indentured to trades and the girls went into service. On leaving the workhouse, inmates (in particular children) could be given an allowance for clothing or provided with clothes from the building store, although clothes were not given to children going into farm service. The amount of the allowance awarded varied but was usually under 45 shillings, rising to 65 shillings in 1864. In July 1862 John Butcher, an orphan, was awarded the unusual amount of £5 for his clothing. This may have been because he was to enter

Christmas decorations in the dining hall about 1926; the 'picture' on the wall is a dietary plan

the service of Charles Wright, the Union clerk, and required a smarter set of clothing than the inmate going into agricultural or domestic service. The award was sufficiently unusual for the Guardians to have to specifically justify the amount to the Poor Law Board in London. In May 1871 it was discovered that one of the inmates, Edward Graves, who had been resident in the workhouse for 14 years, had recently entered service as a labourer and been found in a destitute condition which would necessitate him being returned to the workhouse if the Guardians did not provide him with an outfit. For the girls going into service it was a local practice for the employer not to pay wages for the first year but to pay for the girl's clothes at the end of the year to enable her to obtain a proper position.

The Guardians would look at all means possible for inmates to leave the workhouse. In May 1878 William Philips and Ann Adcock requested permission to leave with the intention of getting married and living at Mattishall. How they managed to get together is unclear; perhaps they knew each other before entering the workhouse. Both parties had children of their own and the Guardians allowed them to stay behind until Philips could take them out after the marriage to live with them.

Not all placements into service were successful. In December 1878 Emma Hill, age 14, returned to the workhouse after service in what seems to have been a public house. As a result of her re-turn the Guardians resolved in future not to send any female child into service in a public house. Emma does not seem to have been entirely blameless for her return. The schoolmistress, Miss Skinner, refused to readmit her to the workhouse school due to her general insubordinate conduct, and in June she was placed in solitary confinement for 24 hours for refractory conduct. In January 1879 Emma was taken before the magistrates for assaulting other inmates.

As well as placing inmates in service the Guardians also occasionally sanctioned emigration overseas. In July 1879 Lydia Carson and her five children were permitted to emigrate to Canada to join her father. Lydia had been deserted by her husband some three years before and the cost of maintaining the four of them in the workhouse was estimated at £60 a year. The Local Government Board sanctioned payment of £3 13s 4d each and in October that year they sailed for Canada on the *Sardinia*.

Death was of course the other way that an inmate left the workhouse. However, for many they did not go very far, being placed in the burial ground that had been set out in 1785. Funerals were pauper funerals, a hasty journey to the grave site, sometimes via the mortuary. Here they were wrapped in a paper or calico strip and placed in a cheap coffin. These coffins were usually made of ¾-inch red Canada pine and came in three sizes, five foot, four to five foot and under four feet and in some cases had

The burial ground today.

a hinged lid to allow them to be reused, being merely used to transport the body. Initially there was a short burial service at the grave site, few if any of the inmates being allowed to attend, but by 1895 the service was being conducted in the chapel. Many of the graves would have been reused with up to twenty bodies in a grave over the years. The cost of any funeral was not to exceed £1.

Sanitation arrangements in the workhouse were basic, consisting of earth privies and open sewers with cesspools at the corners of the building. In 1849 Rev. Benjamin Barker sent a letter to the Poor Law Board describing the poor nature of the drainage arrangements at Gressenhall; he described how the sewage ran into an open ditch in a field to the east of the building and then down into the river. The Visiting Committee recommended that pipes be laid in the ditch but the motion was defeated and the ditch was instead to be cleaned on a regular basis.

The Guardians were mainly the local landowners. Frederick Walpole Keppel from Lexham Hall was appointed the chairman of the board of Guardians when the Union was formed in 1835 and oversaw the implementation of the many changes required at Gressenhall as a result of the 1834 Poor Law Amendment Act. In April 1852 when he retired the other members of the board described him as an 'English gentleman devoting his time and talent to the benefit of the County'. The board met once a fortnight with numerous committees helping to

THE WORKHOUSE STAFF

There were surprisingly few staff in the workhouse to look after the inmates. A master and matron were in charge of day to day operations of the building, a porter controlled entry to the workhouse and a schoolmaster and schoolmistress taught the children, the subjects being determined by the workhouse chaplain. Also in the building were a shoemaker and tailor, and a number of nurses employed to look after the sick, all usually recruited from amongst the inmates. The inmates' hair was cut by a barber sometimes contracted from the local area or as part of the duties of the porter for which he would be paid extra. All the staff in the workhouse suffered from the stigma of working within the Poor Law System and their lives, like those of the inmates, were constrained by rules and regulations. By 1838 they were instructed to take their meal breaks together in the dining room and not in their own apartments. They were also required to do their washing in the workhouse laundry, though presumably this would have been done by the inmates on their behalf.

carry out the day to day running of the building; the meetings seem to have been conducted very formally. In July 1876 the chairman noted that members of the board were not standing to deliver their motions, or to speak. The board voted that the practice of standing 'should be strictly observed in future'. The meetings were held at the workhouse in a special board room lined with green baize to reduce the noise from the inmates, the floor being covered with a drugget. Alongside the board room was a small room where the inmates waited to be called before the board. Contrast this room with the bare white-washed walls and bare floors of the inmates' dormitories. The staff rooms were slightly better, with paper on the walls and more furniture. The workhouse building was also the central point of the Union administration system and was used to store items for the Union such as coffins.

What were the feelings of those living in the surrounding villages towards the workhouse? In October 1846, the chairman, Frederick Walpole Keppel, sent a letter to W. B. Donne in Mattishall:

If you pass Gressenhall Workhouse you must not be startled at hearing 'The Roast Beef of Old England' played before hungry paupers about to be revived with watery gruel, such is the love of mankind for cruelty.

Many local people would not go near the building, preferring to walk the long way round the village to go to the local town of Dereham.

5 Education and Punishment

THE UNION system had been in operation at Gressenhall for 14 years by 1850 and during that period an average of 325 inmates had been accommodated in the building, a lot less than the 560 allowed for by the Poor Law Board. The Guardians could however, claim some success with the children. Between 1845 and 1853, 88 boys had left the workhouse school and found employment. Amongst the professions they entered were shoemaker, tailor, gentleman's service and farm service, the later being the most numerous. Three of the boys became schoolmasters having been used as pupil teachers at Gressenhall.

Down on Union Farm things were not going so well for the tenant, Samuel Pearce. In April 1850, he had been refunded ten pounds due to a misunderstanding in the terms of his lease. The following year he approached the Guardians with a view to having his rent reduced. This was seen as an ideal opportunity to provide an area for the setting up of an Industrial Farm to train the boys. By November an area of 11 acres, called 'Mill Piece' was allocated. Believed to be where the windmill (demolished in 1837) was situated, the area was behind and to the side of the main building. The original intention had been to use the boys to dig this area by hand; however, the ground was so hard, having

previously been growing wheat, that they had to resort to using a plough, presumably borrowed from Samuel Pearce. The number of boys working on the farm averaged 25, assisted by two or three of the older men from the workhouse. The Farm Committee were very pleased that they managed to make a profit during the first year, mainly by selling the produce grown, potatoes and corn, to the workhouse, though they thought that accounting for the labour was unfair as the boys were considered 'totally unproductive to the Union' before the farm was set up. Two years later some thirty boys had been trained to use spades, hoes, forks etc. and been instructed in the management of various kinds of crops. The committee were considering the purchase of two cows to give instruction to girls in dairy work. It is interesting to see that the Guardians were training pupils for life in agriculture, although one would have thought that many of the children would already be conversant with activities such as milking and hoeing, coming as most of them did from an agricultural background. The crops grown at this time on the Industrial Farm included cabbages, wheat, barley, turnips, potatoes and mangels.

Attitudes towards the older inmates, who were in the workhouse through no fault of their own, had softened a little by 1853. In February the

Aerial view of the buildings in 1974. Note the boiler room and chimney, and the remains of the piggeries to the right.

board recommended the building of a separate building to allow elderly married couples to live together. Constructed in the old women's yard by Mr Hubbard of Dereham at a cost of £66 10s 0d, the building had bedrooms for six married couples plus a sitting room and was later to be called Cherry Tree Cottage.

The pond in the workhouse grounds, formed when the clay was dug out to provide the bricks for the original building, must have been a favourite place for the inmates to congregate in their rare moments of leisure. However it did present a hazard: on the 15 July 1853 Cornelius Lusher, an inmate, was found drowned in the pond. Later in May 1861 the Workhouse messenger, Samuel Parker, also drowned in the pond. The subsequent inquest found that 'such act of self destruction was committed under the influence of temporary insanity'.

The workhouse was not a prison and adult inmates could leave at any time after giving suitable notice; however, this did not apply to the orphan children, as they were wards of the Guardians. In July 1855 two boys absconded from the workhouse by climbing over the wall. George White and Elijah Holiday, aged 13, proceeded to visit Lynn, Norwich and various other places in the county. It sounds as if they decided to have a short holiday; unfortunately, this was soon over as on their return they received four days on bread and water. At the time a warrant had been issued against George's mother for failing to maintain him and accusing her of being 'an idle and disorderly person under the Vagrancy Act'. Elijah or Elisha Holiday had been born at Weasenham St Peter and had been in the workhouse for over five years. The following year he requested permission to go to sea and joined a Captain Ridley from South Shields on the ship *Venice*. However, Elijah seems to have suffered an injury because by February 1856 he is reported as being in

These wooden blocks once formed the floor of the boys' schoolroom.

Yarmouth workhouse from where he was transported back to Gressenhall. A month later he is again in trouble for destroying a quantity of oakum.

The boys' schoolroom was in the east wing of the main building. In September 1855 the floor of the room was covered with wooden blocks at a cost of £12. The work was carried out by a Henry Moore, and consisted of hexagonal blocks, believed to be poplar, some 12 inches in depth. The men employed were accommodated in the building, and because of the high standard of work the Guardians did not deduct maintenance from their wages. In 2001 during the upgrade of the Rural Life Museum, the remains of these wooden blocks were found under the floor of the room and are now on show.

Relieving Officers and Overseers were often so keen to place unmarried mothers in the workhouse that they placed the unfortunates in danger. On 16th June 1856 Lucy Bridges from East Dereham was admitted into Gressenhall in such an advanced state of pregnancy that she had to be conveyed in a closed carriage. On the way Lucy started to have labour pains in the carriage and within an hour of being admitted had given birth to a still-born child. Lucy being very ill, she remained in the workhouse infirmary, unfortunately dying on 23rd. The subsequent investigation by the Guardians found that Mr Philo, the Assistant Overseer for East Dereham, was guilty of great neglect in giving the order for Lucy's removal to the workhouse without consulting a medical officer.

The medical officers were always concerned at the general health of the inmates, in particular the children. In March 1860 Dr Vincent felt that the younger boys were suffering from ophthalmia for want of outdoor exercise. Mr Bradfield, the schoolmaster, was instructed to take the boys out for regular walking exercise for at least an hour and a half on three days a week. Bradfield stated that he had been unable to do this before as he had been attending to the older boys working on the Industrial Farm. The unhealthy state of the boys in comparison with the girls was still of concern some four years later and again Bradfield was directed to take the boys out for a walk three days a week for at least an hour. In addition they were also to be taken out each Sunday for a walk in the country and attendance at the local parish church.

Throughout the 1850s and 1860s a number of female inmates were continually in trouble with the workhouse authorities. The most notorious was Harriet Kettle, a short, coarse-faced woman, born in Cranworth near Watton around 1839. Harriet, together with her younger sister Matilda, had become an inmate of the workhouse by 1851 and was a difficult inmate right from the start, repeatedly in trouble with the schoolmistress, Miss Harriet Perfect; she spend a lot of her early time at the workhouse in solitary confinement.

In September 1852 she was sent to prison for 14 days for 'disorderly and insubordinate conduct'. Two months later she was back in prison, this time for 21 days. Harriet was again in trouble in January 1853, when along with two other inmates, Martha and Elizabeth Craske, she was sent to prison for 42 days for 'destroying the food and other property of the Guardians and by wilfully disobeying the orders of the Master and by making a great noise and disturbance and by using obscene and violent language'. Harriet was a perpetually violent and disruptive inmate; two years later she was again in prison for another 42 days. In January 1856 she refused to perform a task ordered by the master and again a fortnight later was sent before the magistrates for 'threatening and violent conduct towards the officers of the House'. The court sentenced her to 21 days in the House of Correction at Little Walsingham. Here she was deemed to be insane because of her violent behaviour and removed to the County Lunatic Asylum at Thorpe near Norwich. This was to be the first of her many removals to the asylum.

By February of the following year Harriet had been released from Thorpe and was requesting outdoor relief from the Guardians. Despite apprehension of her violent behaviour, the Guardians felt that she should return to the workhouse, a view endorsed by the Home Office.

For the next two years, Harriet by her standards seems to have behaved herself, only being reprimanded by the chairman on a number of occasions for violent and abusive language towards the staff. However in November 1858 she was again taken before the magistrates, this time for attempting to set fire to the workhouse. Having been indicted she was found to be insane and transferred to Thorpe. During the Summer Assizes the following year Harriet was again brought to court but her violent language and manner meant that she was immediately sent back to Thorpe. The Guardians' clerk attended the Winter Assizes in December that year only to find that although Harriet had been declared fit to stand trial she had not been discharged from the asylum. However, by January 1860 Harriet was considered of sound mind and on 21 March she finally appeared at the Spring Assizes standing defiantly in the dock declaring that she would take her own life and that 'no man should conquer her'. Upon being asked if she was guilty or not, she straight away launched into a torrent of words, the gist of which was that she did not wish to burn the building down but to kill herself. She maintained that she had been badly treated by the staff at the workhouse, and by others.

The workhouse master, Robert Scraggs, gave evidence that on 2nd November 1858 he had been called to a disturbance in the dining room. On arriving he had found both Harriet and Martha Craske assaulting the assistant matron, Mrs Butcher. Harriet was forcibly removed to

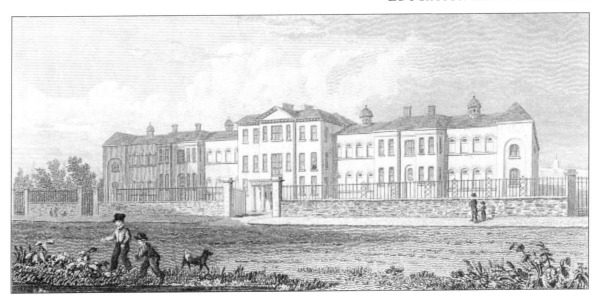

Thorpe Lunatic Asylum in the 1820s

a dormitory room, declaring she would burn the building down. On returning to the room ten minutes later, the master found a quantity of straw which had been ripped from a bed, on fire in the middle of the floor. The fire was put out and Harriet was removed to the magistrates. Expert testimony came from the master of Thorpe Lunatic Asylum, Mr Owen, who stated that although Harriet had been sent to the asylum three times before he did not consider her insane but that she was subject to violent fits of passion especially when she was thwarted. On the other hand the surgeon at Norwich Castle prison, Mr Masters, thought that she was insane. The judge in summing up thought that Harriet was behaving in a violent manner in order to appear insane to escape punishment. The jury agreed and she was sentenced to 18 months hard labour at the House of Correction at Wymondham. This hard labour meant that Harriet was employed in picking oakum, washing, ironing, mending and mat making, tasks she would have been very familiar with at Gressenhall.

A month later the medical authorities at Wymondham once again certified Harriet as insane and committed her to Thorpe and once again Mr Owen was not convinced and sent to the Guardians a certificate of sanity. Over the next few months correspondence passed between the Guardians, the asylum at Thorpe, the House of Correction at Wymondham and the Secretary of State at the Home Office regarding

Harriet and her state of mind. In September the Secretary of State, Sir George Lewis, requested that Harriet be removed from Wymondham and asked the Guardians to recommend another suitable prison to which she could be sent. The Guardians naturally suggested that she should be sent to one outside the county. The following month the Secretary of State wrote that he did not think it necessary to remove Harriet from Wymondham. However, in April the following year she was again certified and removed to Thorpe. By August Harriet had been transferred to the government asylum at St George's in the Fields, London as a criminal lunatic.

Two months later the Guardians received a letter that must have made their hearts sink. According to her sister Matilda, Harriet had been discharged from St George's and was now living with friends in Norwich. After much soul searching the Guardians reluctantly paid out relief if only to 'avoid recurrence of any exciting cause for further violence or mental disease'.

Harriet seems to have kept out of the workhouse until January 1863 but within days of being admitted she was in trouble and again it seemed to be connected with her violent dislike of the assistant matron, Mrs Butcher. The antagonism was such that Mrs Butcher's husband, Thomas, the workhouse porter, had to accompany his wife when she locked up at night to protect her from Harriet.

In April Harriet was allowed to leave the workhouse and reside in Dereham receiving out relief. Some time in the next year it appears that Harriet was again removed to Thorpe, finally being discharged recovered in May 1864. The following year in June she married William Head, an agricultural labourer residing in Dereham. Due to her history and the fact that William was under contract as a team man living with his master, Harriet's out relief continued, much to the dissatisfaction of the Dereham Guardians and parish officers. Harriet was now 26 and as a result of phthisis (pulmonary tuberculosis) was never free of a cough and frequently spat blood. According to the workhouse medical officer her state of mind had not improved – she suffered from what he called 'moral insanity' – and he felt that if she was again placed in the workhouse it would aggravate her mental disease. By the end of the month the Poor Law Board had agreed to the continued payment of out relief.

Harriet then disappears from the minute books; to the probable relief of the Guardians the 1871 Census records her living with her husband in Dereham along with two children, Matilda and Ernest William. Ten years later she and William are living at Cowpers Cottages, Georges Yard, Cowper Road, Dereham together with their children Matilda, 15 (presumably named after Harriet's sister), Ernest W., 13, Alice, 9, and Laura, 7.

Although Harriet was the most notorious inmate

at Gressenhall she was by no means the only girl to cause the Guardians trouble. Martha Craske was a contemporary of Harriet and was involved in two of the instances of misbehaviour along with Harriet. Martha had been born in East Dereham around 1827 and by 1845 was an inmate of the workhouse where she was to spend some 16 years. During that time she was frequently punished for misbehaviour, assault and the use of threatening language. The Guardians' minute books show that Martha was sent to prison on a least 13 occasions. In November 1858 Martha was involved in the assault on Mrs Butcher which saw both Martha and Harriet Kettle being sent to the magistrates. Harriet, of course, was to be charged with attempting to set light to the workhouse. Our researches have yet to reveal what sentence Martha received but it was probably more time in prison. After August 1861, when Martha was again sent to the magistrates for 'gross misbehaviour', Martha disappears from the records of the Guardians.

Elizabeth Neave was another inmate frequently in trouble with the workhouse authorities. Like Martha, Elizabeth was charged with 'violent and disorderly conduct', 'obstinately refusing to work', 'destroying property' and assault during her four years in the workhouse.

Another female inmate in the workhouse during the 1860s was Fanny Roslin. Fanny, apart from numerous instances of refractory conduct, was also charged in December 1864 with indecent behaviour in the workhouse. It appears that she had formed a liaison with another inmate, James Christmas, the two of them having been caught together on two occasions. Three years later Fanny was again in trouble, this time for stealing items from the workhouse stores. Fanny had been admitted to the workhouse as a deserted woman and belonged to the parish of Beeston.

Eliza Steward also came from Beeston and like the others was frequently in trouble with the workhouse authorities. In July 1865 she is described as 'an old offender' when being sent to the magistrates for misbehaviour. Prison does not seem to have had much of an effect on her conduct for on being released from Wymondham she almost immediately re-offended. In July 1866 Eliza found a situation for herself in Wisbech and left the workhouse.

Mary Ann Tennant was another violent and disorderly inmate of the workhouse. In 1857 she was sent before the magistrates for absconding with workhouse clothing. The other girls involved at the time were given refractory punishment; Mary, because she had been in trouble before, was given a prison sentence. In June 1859 she left the workhouse to go into service at Bradenham, but by December she was back at Gressenhall being charged with 'disorderly and violent behaviour'. The Guardians were sufficiently magnanimous to defer her punishment to allow her to partake of Christmas dinner.

Two years later Mary was again in trouble for misbehaving. After that nothing further appears in the Guardians' minute books until June 1874 when she complains to the Guardians about the conduct of the schoolmistress towards her

CLIMBING BOYS

The Guardians were always on the look-out for situations in which to place the children from the workhouse. By 1862 some 127 children had been educated and placed into service; however, their zeal sometimes led them to placing a child in unsuitable employment. In December 1860 it was proposed that Robert Foulsham, an orphan 10 years old, born in Brisley, be placed with Mr Christopher Chapman Sainty of Hingham, a chimney sweep. Other Guardians at the meeting were concerned that it was now illegal to employ boys for climbing up chimneys and that it would be improper for the board to sanction this style of employment for Robert. The third Chimney Sweep Act of 1846 had banned climbing boys under 21 but was still being ignored by most people. However by a vote of 6 to 4 the Guardians agreed to allow the boy to enter Mr Sainty's service. The chairman of the board, Philip Gurdon, was not happy with the outcome of the vote and in a handwritten minute protested at the illegality of the resolution. At the next meeting the Guardians realised they were making an error and withdrew the proposition. Three years later Charles Kingsley published his novel *The Water Babies* which highlighted the plight of the climbing boys and finally led to the practice dying out in the 1870s.

cousin Mary Charlish. The complaint was dismissed by the Guardians and Mary was admonished on the 'impropriety of her conduct'.

In May 1863 George Barker of Bawdeswell and Edward Boyce, both from Gressenhall, were taken before the magistrates having absconded from the house at night. Edward had been born in 1848 and frequently appears in the workhouse punishment book charged with refractory conduct. The Guardians on a number of times attempted to place him in a situation, until finally in September 1863 he went to work for Mr James Nicholson at Gressenhall. Nicholson was a Guardian and also chairman of the Farm Committee, so was ideally placed to see Edward's worth as a labourer.

Relieving the burden on the poor rates was of major concern to the Guardians. In some cases they even agreed that wives or children could be left behind in the workhouse while the husband or mother went into service. Mary Ann Andrews, a single mother from Horningtoft, was one such example. Resident at Gressenhall for the previous four years, Mary in February 1864 had the prospect of gaining respectable employment, but this was at risk as she had a child. The Guardians allowed the child to remain at Gressenhall with Mary paying maintenance of a shilling a week.

Although conditions in the workhouse seem to be bad, in many cases they were better than those of the agricultural labourers outside. In September 1864 the infant child of Christopher

Interior of the chapel

High from Oxwick was admitted to the work-house. The Highs lived in a two-room house, one room of which was used as a kitchen the other as the bedroom. This bedroom was only nine foot by seven foot and had only one bed, in which the father slept. His seven children, the three oldest being 15, 13 and 11, the later being girls, slept on straw on the floor. Christopher had recently lost his wife and the Guardians gave an order for the whole family to enter the workhouse but did allow the father and eldest son to decline entry to allow them to continue at work. In November Christopher reappeared before the board to inform them that a private charity had now provided proper bed and clothing for the children and he was allowed to take his children out of the workhouse except the infant, promising to pay sixpence a week towards its maintenance.

At Gressenhall, religious services were still being conducted in the dining room between 9 and 11 o'clock in the morning and 2 and 4 o'clock in the afternoon. This was obviously difficult to arrange around the feeding of the inmates. What was needed was a separate building and in 1867 a proposal to build a chapel was voted in by 25 to 13, the building to be paid for by private subscription. Designed by R. M. Phipson, Norfolk's County Surveyor, the chapel was erected during 1868 and officially opened on 2nd December. The opening was considered such an event that a substantial tea was provided by the master for the inmates, with sausage rolls and bread and butter. The pork for the sausages came from the Industrial Farm's own pigs. The chapel was licensed for the performance of divine service and for administering the sacraments of Baptism and the Lord's Supper.

During March 1868 the Guardians became concerned that the administration of the workhouse was suffering as a result of Mr and Mrs Scraggs, the master and matron, being seriously ill. Mrs Scraggs unfortunately died on 21st and the Guardians awarded Mr Scraggs a sum of £25 towards the cost of the funeral. By the end of the month the Guardians received an offer from a Mr and Mrs Horne, previously porter and assistant matron at Gressenhall from 1863, to act as a temporary master and matron until Mr Scraggs' condition necessitated the appointment of a permanent replacement. Scraggs finally resigned in April and Philip John Reynolds and his wife Beloy Ann Lucy were appointed to the posts.

Contact between officers and inmates on anything other than an official basis were actively discouraged. However, living in such close confinement liaisons probably occurred. On 20th April 1868 Elizabeth Rudd, a female inmate, gave birth to a baby girl. Elizabeth already had four other illegitimate children but this one was different, as she claimed that the father was the workhouse schoolmaster, Robert Bradfield, who strenuously denied the allegation. According to her statement at the subsequent enquiry the seduction had taken place the previous June in Bradfield's rooms which she was employed to clean together with the boys' bedrooms at the workhouse. Bradfield earlier in his career at Gressenhall had gained a reputation for leaving the house without permission for unspecified 'pleasures' in Dereham and this may have been a contributing factor in Elizabeth's accusations. The enquiry, conducted by Lt Col P. B. Ward, the Poor Law Inspector, found that there was no case against Bradfield and his name was cleared. Born around 1819 in Brisley, Bradfield had become the schoolmaster at Gressenhall in March 1840 at the age of 19. Despite his young age he soon earned a reputation as a very good teacher and was responsible for training two pupil teachers, William Seaman and William Parker. Bradfield tendered his resignation in May 1874 after 34 years' service at Gressenhall, receiving a testimonial that he had 'conducted his duties in a manner most satisfactory to the Guardians while his general character and conduct has been unimpeachable'. The Guardians put his resignation down to a 'natural desire to retire from the monotony of an employment in which he had been engaged for so many years'. But how much was due to the furore of the Elizabeth Rudd affair?

6 Improving Conditions

BY THE 1870s, workhouses were seeing increasing numbers of sick and infirm paupers being admitted, leading many Boards of Guardians to add or convert existing buildings into purpose-built infirmaries. At Gressenhall the Guardians employed the services of Mr Albert Kelly, an architect living in Dereham, to come up with a design for an infirmary. The early proposals consisted of an entirely new building; however, by October after further deliberations that decision had been reversed and plans to convert the east wing of the existing building were drawn up by Mr Kelly at a cost of £21. Work started on converting the wing in April 1871, funded by a loan of £2,000 obtained from the Public Works Loan Board to be paid back over the next ten years. The work was carried out by William Hubbard from Dereham and was finished in June the following year.

Whilst the building work on the new infirmary was being carried out, the aged paupers were restricted from being allowed outside the walls onto the pleasure ground, the series of broad walks which had been laid out in 1837. The loss of this privilege led to some indignation on their part and a letter was received by the Poor Law Board from a Mr John Egerton Webster, complaining of the conduct of Mr Reynolds, the master, towards the aged paupers. The allegation was unsubstantiated and in fact the aged paupers in the workhouse denied ever having any correspondence with Mr Webster, one, Robert Middleton, 'emphatically denying that he had ever written the letter bearing his name'. With the completion of the building work the old men were once again allowed their liberty and by December 1880 they were able to go onto the grounds in front of the house between 9 o'clock and 11 o'clock in the morning and 2 o'clock and 4 o'clock in the afternoon. However, the gate onto the highway was kept locked and manned, probably by the porter.

Also built at the same time as the infirmary was a separate bungalow along the south wall which acted as a fever and isolation ward. In October 1876 this was occupied by the children of James Ayres from Gressenhall. The Ayres family of six children had been living in an overcrowded house with only one sleeping compartment. With the children in the fever ward a nurse was employed to live in and look after them.

With all the extra building work and alterations, the Guardians were becoming increasingly concerned at the quantity of water that was available to the workhouse. In January 1865 the main well in the courtyard in front of the building had been deepened; it was further deepened in 1874 as a result of the extra

Postcard of about 1910, showing the east wing, converted in 1871 to house the infirmary.

requirements for the new infirmary. The following year the clerk was asked to look into the possibility of extracting by hydraulic rams water from the river running below the farm. Nothing came of his investigation and it was not until 1901 that a ram house was built to supply water from the river up the hill to the workhouse which by February 1904 was taking some 50,000 gallons (227,300 litres) of water a day from the river.

The rules allowing inmates to discharge themselves were changed in July 1873. If the inmate had not been discharged previously in the month, they could now leave at 24 hours' notice. If they had been discharged before in the month they had to give two days' notice and if they had been frequently discharged during the month they were required to give three days' notice. This seems to show that many inmates were in and out of the workhouse. Also that month the medical officer was recommending

an allowance of two pints of beer daily to each inmate engaged on the more laborious tasks in the workhouse. Amongst these tasks were washing, cooking, grave-digging, funerals and emptying privies and drains.

Like many workhouses at the time, Gressenhall housed a number of people classified as imbeciles. In 1874 some 19 of these unfortunates were accommodated amongst the 200 inmates. The cost to the Guardians for keeping them at Gressenhall was around six shillings a week. To send them to the County Asylum at Thorpe would have cost 9s 2d a week, of which four shillings was paid for by government grant. As a result those inmates considered manageable were kept at Gressenhall and only when they became unmanageable or annoying to other inmates were they sent to Thorpe.

The Local Government Board in London, who had taken over administration of the Poor Law from the Poor Law Board in 1871, occasionally received letters from inmates complaining of conditions or their treatment. Few of the inmates could of course write, but occasionally some professional people fell on hard times and were forced to enter the workhouse. One such was John Butcher, a solicitor's clerk who knew his rights and entitlements as an inmate. In June 1874 he had been taken before a magistrate and convicted of misbehaviour in the workhouse, having broken a window in his ward. Butcher's excuse was that the porter had been an hour late in unlocking the ward to let the inmates out for the day. Later that month he complained at his treatment to the Local Government Board, a month later again writing to the Guardians complaining at the loss of some of his privileges and alterations in his diet. He received little sympathy from either the Local Government Board or the Guardians, who considered themselves justified in withholding the privileges as Butcher had committed numerous offences.

By 1874 the Industrial Farm had begun to experience problems with only nine boys working. The master, Philip Reynolds, did not have the time to supervise them and Francis Gale, the schoolmaster, was considered by James Nicholson, the chairman of the Farm Committee, 'totally ignorant of the required cultivation of the land'. As a result the original eight acres called 'Mill Piece' were returned to the Union Farm tenant, the Industrial Farm now only oc-

cupying some two and half acres adjoining the building. The Industrial Farm continued to operate throughout the life of the workhouse, in later years tending to be given over to the rearing of pigs, although how much waste would have been generated from the meagre rations given to the inmates is a subject for speculation. The enterprise did however manage to make a yearly profit of between £85 0s 9d in 1860 to £21 13s 3d in 1902. Union Farm itself at this time consisted of over 51 acres (20.6 hectares) of arable and pasture land and was being leased by George Pearce. The Pearce family had held the tenancy since 1840, first by Samuel, then his wife Elizabeth for a while, then her executors and now George. The effect of the agricultural depression in the country can be seen by the fall in rent of the farm from £129 a year in 1840 to £80 a year in 1875. George Pearce also supplied milk to the workhouse, but by October 1878 the Guardians were concerned that the milk being supplied was adulterated with water. Pearce admitted the practice but claimed that this had been 'customary for many years'. He was ordered to supply the milk at a price of 2d per pint and at the end of the current quarter to supply at 1d per pint; this he was unable to do and the Guardians had to look for another supplier.

Life in the workhouse could be interrupted by activities which, although considered petty by the Guardians, had a major impact on the inmates' lives. An example of this occurred in February of 1876 when the old and infirm inmates complained to the Guardians of the quality of pea soup and tea that they were receiving. The master, Philip Reynolds, admitted that the pea soup had been improperly cooked and that the tea was also of inferior quality and also admitted that he had supplied some 11oz (312 grams) of tea less than that prescribed by the dietary tables. A week later Reynolds was called before the board and 'admonished to excise more careful supervision in future'.

The entry recording this event in the Guardians' minute book also gives a fascinating glimpse of life in the workhouse. A proposal was put forward to discontinue the practice of allowing the women to cook food for their children during the usual Sunday visits. This cooking seems to have been carried out in the laundry, as the Guardians banned fires in this area. The following month the board received a letter from the Local Government Board regarding alleged mistreatment of the aged and infirm inmates' diet. These allegations had appeared in a newspaper and the Guardians invited the Poor Law Inspector, Mr Boyle, to investigate. After spending several hours at Gressenhall, Mr Boyle reported that the complaints of the aged and infirm regarding their diet and the alleged neglect by the medical officer and other officials 'were not justified by the evidence'. The clerk was directed to write to the editors of the various papers that had published the allegations to inform them of the result of Mr Boyle's investigations.

The nurses employed at the workhouse seemed to vary in their capabilities. In December 1876 Miss Helen Hart from Sparkbrook was appointed as nurse having been the sole applicant for the vacant position. By the following month the Guardians had received a letter from the Local Government Board enclosing copies of a letter from her previous employers detailing her previous unsatisfactory service. Dr Vincent, Gressenhall's own medical officer, obviously agreed for he found Nurse Hart 'to be very inefficient, (almost dangerous), careless and negligent in not personally seeing that the patients are keep clean'. Hart was instantly dismissed that day.

Tragedy struck the workhouse in the early hours of 1st April 1878. Sarah Hemsell, an aged imbecile pauper, in attempting to escape from the female infirmary ward fell from an upper window. Despite her injuries she managed to crawl some distance along the adjacent road before she was discovered dead at 4.30 in the morning. The coroner's inquest recorded a verdict of 'death by accidentally falling from a window in the workhouse' and recommended the fitting of iron bars to the upstairs windows.

Frank Roach, the schoolmaster in 1876, seems to have been a very ambitious man. In May 1878 he unsuccessfully applied for an appointment as schoolmaster with the Brighton Union. His work at Gressenhall was, however, appreciated by the Inspector, H. C. Bowyer, who reported that he was very pleased with the boys' school 'which is highly creditable to the Master'. In August both Roach and Elizabeth Martha Skinner, the schoolmistress at Gressenhall, jointly applied for the vacant office of master and matron at the Pulham St Mary workhouse in Norfolk, again unsuccessfully. Roach had obviously formed some form of partnership with Elizabeth Skinner as in November 1879 both applied for the post of schoolmaster and schoolmistress at the Faversham Union workhouse; in this they were presumably successful because in December Charles Eastoe from Litcham was elected as schoolmaster at Gressenhall.

Eastoe seems to have had difficulty fitting in. In September 1880 he is complaining about the conduct of the master, Philip Reynolds, towards himself and requesting to be allowed to eat his meals in his own rooms. Reynolds' attitude towards the schoolmaster seems to have stemmed from the fact that Eastoe was paying attentions to his daughter Fanny. The case was investigated by Mr Courtney Boyle, the Local Government Board Inspector, in October and Eastoe was told that if he continued his unwelcome attentions to Fanny he would be dismissed. Three months later one of the boys, George Bartram, complained that he had been injured by Eastoe, who was admonished to adhere strictly to the Local Government Board rules for administering corporal punishment. The following month

it was the turn of the chaplain to lay a complaint against the schoolmaster and in April 1881 Eastoe attended before the Guardians to report that someone, he believed it to be the master or matron, had entered his rooms and taken some letters, supposedly written between Fanny and himself. Both the master and Mrs Reynolds denied the charge, but a month later Fanny resigned her post as the schoolmistress, Eastoe himself only remaining until September when he was given notice to leave.

By March 1881 the Guardians were starting to look seriously at boarding out the children with suitable families in the parishes. This system was in use at some of the other Unions in Norfolk and it was felt that it would be a way of closing the workhouse schools to save money. The Guardians agreed to pay for each child at a cost of four shillings a week and to kit them out with an outfit of clothes. For some reason the Guardians did not board out children to people living in East Dereham. By December 1882 some 13 children, 9 girls and 4 boys, had been boarded out. These children were regularly visited by members of the committee as well as the local clergy and medical officers.

After the departure of Eastoe the separate boys' and girls' schools in the workhouse were amalgamated into one mixed school with the children now under the supervision of a schoolmistress, Miss Mary Ann Taylor from East Dereham. Mary seems to have been unable

Children at Gressenhall village school, in a picture taken before 1914. The boys on the right are probably from the workhouse; note their shaven heads.

to cope with running the mixed school and resigned in March 1882, although the Guardians considered her a 'competent teacher in the Girls School'. Over the next two years four schoolmistresses were appointed, none lasting for more than a year with all of them seeming to have problems in maintaining discipline in the mixed school. The last of these, Elizabeth Haythorpe, was given notice to quit after a visit by the Local Government Board Inspector found 'the workhouse school in a most unsatisfactory state, the reading writing and arithmetic of the children being equally bad'. As early as 1883

the Guardians had looked at sending the children to the local village schools at Gressenhall and Beetley and in August 1884 some 40 children were sent to Gressenhall school. However, by January 1887 the children were back in the workhouse. Part of the problem was the behaviour of some of the boys at Gressenhall school, in particular George Farrer, who was allegedly excessively chastised by the schoolmaster; however, on investigation it was found that both George and his brother William's conduct had been bad, severely provoking the schoolmaster. As a result the school managers suggested that the workhouse children would no longer be welcome at the school and a schoolmistress, Miss Elizabeth Laister, was again appointed at the workhouse. The school at this time contained some 60 children and to help ease the load an Infant schoolmistress: Mary Ann Stephenson was appointed to teach those children between the ages of three and five.

A further attempt was made in 1896 to send the children out of the workhouse to local schools but the managers of Gressenhall school still objected. The Guardians also looked at sending the boys to Hartismere school in the Wortham Union in Suffolk, but this proposal came to nothing. Eventually in June 1898 Rev. J. M. Ward at Gressenhall school consented to a limited number of boys being admitted, the girls being sent to Beetley school, and the workhouse schools were finally closed. The infants under five who remained were still taught by the Infant schoolmistress until 1899 when the post became that of caretaker and general assistant. Miss Melton, the last Infant schoolmistress, accepted the lower grade post but only for two months.

Reading through the Guardians' minute books, we see certain inmates appearing before the board with regularity. We have already looked at some of the female inmates but what of the men? Robert Pitcher was one such inmate always in trouble. Born in Shipdham around 1834, by the time he was 45 he found himself in Gressenhall workhouse along with his wife Elizabeth. Robert was a general labourer and had difficulty in finding work, presumably because of his attitude, he frequently using threatening language to staff and other inmates. In August 1880 this expanded into an actual assault on another inmate, Thomas Boyce, during a disturbance in the infirmary, which resulted in him being sent to prison for seven days. The following month Robert seems to have been the only able-bodied man at Gressenhall, as he was complaining of being locked up alone in his ward. During the next two years he continued to be in trouble for using threatening language and refusing to pick oakum. On two occasions in 1884 Robert and a female inmate, Mary Knoll, were reprimanded for improper behaviour. The minute book does not detail the full nature of the offence but it is to be assumed that Elizabeth, his wife, who was ten years older, was no longer alive. Nothing further is recorded about Robert for another two years when he is again sent to prison for 21 days for assaulting another inmate. Later that same year, in October 1886, he is again sent to prison for assault, this time for 14 days. A month later a fight took place in the infirmary between Robert and another inmate, Robert Palmer, employed as a wardsman.

In January 1887 the Guardians received a letter from a Mr Walter Pitcher from Milton, Ontario, Canada asking for help in allowing his brother Robert Pitcher to emigrate to Canada. It is uncertain whether this is the same Robert

Pitcher that had been causing all the trouble in the workhouse. If it was he was now over 50 years old and it would be strange if he was considered a candidate for emigration. However, despite this, in July 1887 Robert duly arrived in Canada. It would have been hoped by the Guardians that this was the last they would see of Robert, but it was not to be. In August 1896 the clerk presented before the board a warrant for the removal of a Robert Pitcher from Glasgow back to Gressenhall. It is possible that this is the same Robert Pitcher who migrated to Canada, for Glasgow was a major port for ships to and from Canada and the USA. Once back at Gressenhall Robert was soon back to his old tricks, refusing to work and generally misbehaving.

By 1883 the Guardians were becoming aware of a conflict between the matron, Mrs Reynolds and the nurse, Ellen Murray, leading to Murray resigning because of the opposition to her ideas from the matron. A committee was formed to enquire into the administration of the infirmary and after much deliberation changes were made to the management of the infirmary and as a result Nurse Murray withdrew her resignation and continued at Gressenhall until 1899. After visit by the Local Government Board Inspector, Mr Lockwood, in July, the master and matron were censured for their 'lack of inclination or ability to get on with the Officers'.

The Guardians also became concerned at the number of unmarried women coming to the workhouse infirmary to have their babies at the expense of the rate payers. Many of these women were returning five or even seven times to have their children. The solution adopted was to ensure that the women declared the name of the father, who would then be charged for the woman's maintenance whilst in the workhouse. If paternity could not be proved or the woman refused to divulge the child's father's name then she would be taken before a magistrate, who could imprison her for wilful neglect. Even as late as the 1880s unmarried mothers, although no longer required to wear the 'jacket', were still considered immoral and social outcasts.

Sanitation and the prevention of the spread of disease were a continual cause of concern for

Thought to be from the workhouse, this bath was found on the farm being used as a water-trough!

the Guardians. By mid-1885 a number of the children in the workhouse had contracted ringworm. The medical officer was asked by the Guardians for suggestions to prevent its spread. His reply was that the children required as much exercise as possible in the open air and also ensure that their clothes were boiled and washed separately from those of the other inmates. In addition the children's ward was to be disinfected. In September 1886 Henry Read, a two-year-old boy was 'found dead in a privy vault'. At the time serious consideration was given to replacing the privies with the old earth closets to prevent accidents like this occurring again.

May 1887 saw the Jubilee of Queen Victoria, and Mr Thomas Cranmer from East Dereham requested permission to give the inmates a dinner in her honour. The Guardians initially gave their permission but later withdrew it when the Local Government Board gave permission for inmates to be 'regaled in the Workhouse with roast beef and plum pudding in celebration of Her Majesty's Jubilee'. However Mr Cranmer did not give up, and in August was able to treat the old people and children from the workhouse in the grounds of his house, Quebec Hall, in Dereham.

Mr Cranmer was not the only local dignitary to offer treats to the workhouse inmates. Since 1877 Miss Sophia Edwards from Hardingham Lodge had annually allowed the old men and women to spend the day at her residence. The cost of conveying the inmates was generally

paid for by Miss Edwards while local people provided the waggons. Miss Edwards continued to send gifts for the inmates right up until 1929. The Lady Visitors to the workhouse also annually gave a tea to the inmates in January.

In this boiler the clothes of tramps arriving at the workhouse were disinfected.

7 Refuge of Last Resort

THROUGHOUT THE 19th century the Guardians in most of the Norfolk workhouses, including Gressenhall, adopted policies of poor relief that they considered suitable to the conditions in the countryside at the time. By the end of the century few if any able bodied paupers were in residence apart from the casuals, and the workhouse was now becoming a place of last refuge for the sick, elderly and infirm. By 1890 the medical officer at Gressenhall, Henry Vincent, was requesting extra beds for the infirmary and extra nurses to be hired from the nursing home at Fakenham and the Workhouse Infirmary Nursing Association. By February 1896 the infirmary was full, with 80 cases of which 45 were sick and 35 infirm. The medical officer, Mr Arthur Rackham, who had replaced Henry Vincent in 1895, requested that two further trained nurses and a probationer nurse be hired for the infirmary. By 1897 the infirmary was housing 59 inmates out of a total population of 169, and only two nurses were on duty. The night nurse had to rouse her charges at a quarter to four in the morning in order to get through all her work. The nurses had no certificate in midwifery but had dealt with some 35 cases over the previous two years of which they had only called for help from the medical officer in two cases. The government Inspector had also observed an imbecile inmate carrying a two-month-old child, she having not been out of the workhouse for over 18 months.

In 1894 the Mitford and Launditch Rural District Council produced their first annual report for the Ministry of Health. With respect to the workhouse at Gressenhall they reported that 18 males and 6 females had died over the year, 15 of the men being over the age of 65. Some 162 pauper inmates had contracted sickness and there were seven births at the workhouse, six of which were illegitimate. The report considered that the sanitary conditions of the building were fairly good; however, the report's authors considered that the heating of the infirmary was unsatisfactory and very costly. The fire precautions were considered inadequate, both as to the water supply and the means of escape for the sick and elderly inmates.

The chapel had been built in 1868 for Church of England services but by 1892 certain Guardians had become concerned that other denominations were unable to conduct their own services at the workhouse. Mr Benjamin Brett, Guardian for East Dereham, requested that licensed ministers of the Primitive and Wesleyan Methodist, Baptist and Congregationalist churches be allowed to hold evening services either on the workhouse green or in the dining hall on Sundays at a different time from the main Church of England service in the chapel. The proposal was carried and the nonconformists began to hold services in the dining room. They were clearly unhappy about the arrangement and really wished to use the chapel so three years later another proposal was put forward, again being narrowly defeated. However, a second proposal that the nonconformists could use the west end of the chapel on Sunday afternoons was passed.

Up to the last decade of the 19th century burial of inmates was carried out with little ceremony in the workhouse burial ground. A couple of inmates would have dug the grave and the body would have been brought from the mortuary to the grave-side where the chaplain would have read a short service. Mourners from amongst the other inmates were rarely allowed to attend. In August 1895 the Guardians ruled that the body should now be taken from the mortuary (or Dead House) to the chapel where the chaplain was to carry out the full burial ceremony. Inmates were now allowed to attend the service.

The Guardians continued to give assistance to those paupers and inmates requesting emigration. One such was Peace Pratt. Peace had been born in the village of Whissonsett around 1836 and was an inmate of Gressenhall by 1868. The census lists her as a field worker with a daughter of 5, Eliza; she is also recorded as an

The door to the mortuary is much overgrown today.

imbecile. Despite being in trouble a number of times the Guardians considered her harmless and she remained in the workhouse for a number of years. In January 1890 her daughter Eliza wrote to the Guardians requesting assistance in allowing her mother to emigrate to Australia to join another daughter, Alice. Alice sent £25 for her mother's passage and the Guardians agreed to supply an outfit and all other expenses. However, Peace did not stay long in Australia as a year later the daughter arranged for Peace to return to England. She presumably returned to Gressenhall as in 1897 Peace is recorded as being put on bread and water for using profane language.

The small number of staff at Gressenhall meant that sometimes inmates were used to look after the sick and elderly and this could lead to problems. In July 1894 Mr Brett reported to the board that he had received complaints that some of the pauper attendants were ill-treating the old women in the infirmary. No names were given as

KEEPING OUT THE PRESS

The Guardians were reluctant to allow outsiders to attend board meetings. In May 1889 a proposal by William Vincent to allow a newspaper reporter to attend had been rejected by 34 votes to 6 and it was not until December 1894 that the Guardians voted by 21 to 15 to finally allow press coverage of board meetings. Their reluctance to allow reporting of board meetings can be appreciated, for on 10th April 1897 the *Dereham and Fakenham Times* ran a report of a complaint from a 27-year-old pauper from Litcham. He maintained that the porter had knocked him about for complaining about the gruel. The Guardians though had little sympathy for the man, saying that at his age he should be outside earning a living. Press reporting of board meetings continued until 1946 when the County Council decided to ban reporters.

Mr Brett had been informed that the old women had been intimidated. The Visiting Committee investigated and as a result introduced new procedures to prevent any recurrence.

On 2nd September 1897 one of the oldest inmates in the workhouse died. Peter Pentey had been born on 28th June 1796 at Mattishall and worked hard all his life. He had started as a 'copper hole jack' (a stoker) at the age of 8 and later as a navvy on the railways. Married at the age of 26, he had fathered four children, although his wife had died young, and at the age of 96 he was forced to enter Gressenhall. He was a character well respected by the other inmates and the Guardians, and was to be seen daily smoking his pipe and watching the children playing. His last prayer before he died peacefully was 'Oh Lord take me home'; he was buried in the workhouse burial ground.

Philip Reynolds had been master at Gressenhall since 1868 and retired in 1896. Soon after his retirement a report appeared in the local paper under the title 'Workhouse Administration Criticised'. At a previous board meeting the government Inspector, Mr P. H. Bagenal, had reported on the need for a hot water supply, the lack of facilities for tramps to dry their clothing, and the fact that they were being detained for two nights. He also commented on the inadequate supply of linen. Reynolds had been warned by the Inspector on a previous visit not to place so many inmates into rooms. Twelve men were being accommodated in a room designed to take only six and twelve women in a space for only nine. The Guardians were also concerned that no handkerchiefs were being given to the young and old. One Guardian considered it essential that the children should be sent out into service with handkerchiefs as they were a 'rudimentary element of civilisation'.

The report in the paper quoted the chairman, Mr Copeman, as saying that 'they were in charge of the largest and most disgraceful house in Norfolk' and considered that in Charles Henry Knight 'they now had a good Master and should keep him'. The Guardians also considered that 'discipline in the house had gone down to a very low ebb' under Reynolds' administration. The attitude of the Guardians in this matter is curious as previously in May 1897 when the Mr and Mrs Reynolds had retired they had considered them to have carried out their duties in an 'efficient way'. Criticism of Reynolds' administration had previously appeared in the local papers in March 1896 when he was accused of mis-accounting with regard to the supply of seeds to the workhouse garden. At the time the case was dropped and Reynolds was exonerated. With these latest allegations Reynolds was naturally very upset and in October 1897 wrote to the *Eastern Daily Press* stating that he had 'endeavoured in dealing with the unfortunate old people by kindness to make the house as much a home as it was possible and tried to make them feel that they were not

prisoners under punishment'. The Guardians did not get their wish in keeping their new master as Knight resigned some eight months later.

Guardians at Gressenhall tended to serve for a number of years. Richard Charles Brown served for 26 years, resigning as chairman in January 1893 through ill health and dying in April. Thomas Henry Hubbard, his replacement, retired as chairman of the board of Guardians in 1899. Hubbard had been chairman for the previous four years and a Guardian for North Elmham for 38 years. Another long-serving member of the Union who retired in 1896 was John Cary. Cary had been the porter at the workhouse between 1841 and 1849 and had been a Relieving and Vaccination Officer for the next 47 years.

Since 1797 inmates who had died in the workhouse had been buried on site. In 1898 the Guardians attempted to build an additional

The porter's lodge, photographed in 1976

burial ground but were prevented by the Local Government Board. By 1900 the existing burial ground was full and the decision was taken to return the bodies of paupers dying in the workhouse to their own village or parish, a hearse being provided to convey the body. However, after 1902 some burials were still being undertaken, mainly of still-born children. In the 1920s some of the bodies of inmates who had died in the workhouse were sent to Cambridge College of Anatomy, but only in those cases where there were no relatives alive. This practice seems to have continued right up until the workhouse closed in 1948. By January 1904 the master had been given permission to level the site and erect a stone tablet on the nearest wall. The tablet was inscribed 'THIS PIECE OF GROUND AND THE PIECE OF GROUND ON THE WEST THEREOF WERE FOR MANY YEARS THE BURIAL GROUND FOR INMATES OF THIS WORKHOUSE AND BURIALS THEREON WERE DISCONTINUED IN 1900'. Today the area has been planted as an orchard and houses some 40 varieties of old apples rescued by the Norfolk Apples and Orchard Project.

Apple trees now grow in the former burial ground.

Throughout its existence Gressenhall had been poorly heated, with few fireplaces in the rooms, apart from those occupied by the staff. By 1890 Henry Vincent, the medical officer, had become concerned and was recommending the installation of a warm water system. The Guardians looked at similar systems in the Aylsham and Downham Market workhouses and plans for installing heating and remodelling the laundry were drawn up Mr Green, the architect, in October 1895 at a cost of £2,870. The following month the Guardians were expressing concern at the cost but were 'fondly hoping that the time is not far distant when our deserving poor shall be spared the pain and dread of having to spend their last days in a Union Workhouse'. The plans were altered in December but put on hold for three months which angered Rev. Henry Collinson. Collinson had made the initial proposal for the alterations and was a passionate champion of the inmates' welfare; as a result of the project being put on hold he resigned from the committee. The matter was referred back and the following month Collinson withdrew his resignation and new plans were sent to the Local Government Board for approval in January. Authority to implement the changes was received in May 1897 with full authority to borrow the £2,750 required. Two years later hot and cold water supplies to the infirmary were implemented and by June 1900 further improvements were introduced with steam power to perform cooking and laundry work. Tenders in 1901 showed work on a new boiler house at the back of the main building, heating hot water for boilers and drying racks. The following year, 1902, further alterations to the workhouse were carried out by Bradfield & Co under plans drawn up by the architect J. B. Pearce, water heaters were purchased to replace older equipment and by September there were two boilers, three water heaters and three engines on site. All this work was carried out with the aid of a loan of £3,650 from the Public Works Loan Board. The washing and drying machines were replaced by electrically driven examples in the 1950s, but the drying racks still survive in the laundry building along with the drives and pulleys from the original steam engine. The introduction of these new boilers and steam engines meant

Drying racks

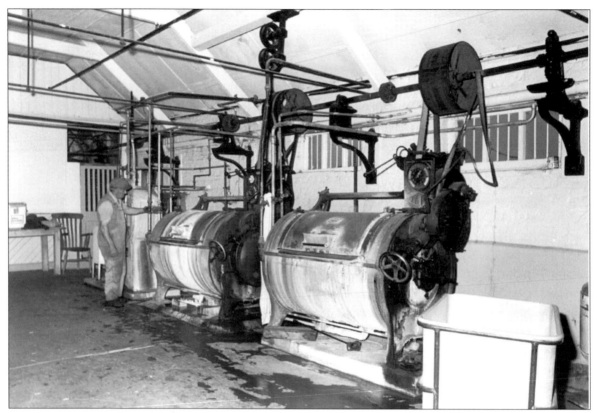

The laundry, photographed in 1974

that from 1903 the Guardians had to employ an engineer, George Neale, to look after the machinery. Neale remained at the workhouse until August 1927 when he resigned after 27 years of service. Aged 54, he had developed tuberculosis and was considered unfit to continue working, and by October had died.

In February 1901 the Guardians recorded their deep sense of loss at the death of Queen Victoria, with a black-lined entry in the minute book. A year later the inmates were presented with a tea on the coronation of Edward VII. The tea included cold beef, ham, salad, tart, beer, ginger beer and tobacco with the inmates being entertained with music. Also in celebration, extra out relief of a shilling for each adult and sixpence for each child in the Union was given out.

The workhouse system was continually under

investigation by Royal Commissions during the early years of the 20th century. In their 1905 report they found that the principles of the 1834 Act had been gradually eroded since the 1880s. Most of the Commission's recommendations were ignored by the government of the day but pressure from various groups did force them to introduce pensions for the over-70s in 1908 and the National Insurance Scheme Act in 1911. These reforms meant that some elderly people then did not to have to enter the workhouse. By January 1913 there were 44 inmates at Gressenhall eligible for the old age pension and those able to leave were given an outfit of clothes to the value of £2. For those inmates forced to stay in the workhouse the Guardians' opinion was that they should pay for their maintenance out of their pensions. In 1907 the Guardians forwarded suggestions to the Royal Commission on the Poor Laws and Relief of Distress that feebleminded and imbecile inmates should be sent to the asylum. They also asked to be given discretionary powers to detain women of immoral character for up to 12 months and that vagrants should be under police control and not allowed into the workhouse.

Gressenhall at the time, like most workhouses, had a high number of elderly inmates. One such was Robert Middleton, age 70, known locally as 'Loafing Been'. In February 1904 he fell out of a chair whilst asleep and broke his leg. Despite being put to bed he proved to be a troublesome and restless patient and gradually

Robert Neville, Master, and family together with other staff members in 1902. Back row: 1 Mr Whitby (Assistant Clerk), 2 Mrs Whitby. Middle row: 1 ?, 2 Mr Neville (Master), 3 baby, 4 Mrs Neville (Matron). Front row: 1 Robert Neville (son), 2 girl (Whitby?)

became weaker before finally dying. Another inmate, Frances Beckett, also met an unfortunate death, having been administered carbolic acid in mistake for Epsom salts. The Guardians recommended that in future coloured ribbed poison bottles be purchased to prevent further 'mistakes'.

Drainage at the workhouse and the disposal of sewage was a constant problem for the Guardians since Rev. Benjamin Barker had raised concerns in 1849 about the open ditch to the east of the building. Further reports on the drainage were made in 1890 and plans for new drainage were approved by the Local Government Board in September 1898. The following year two more filter beds were built at the outfall of the workhouse drainage system, treating the sewage before it entered the river. 1909 saw further concerns about drainage when the Guardians were accused by the City of Norwich Water Works of polluting the river with sewage from the workhouse. Alterations were made to the sewage tank and to the output of water from the laundry by Messrs Neale and Co in June 1910, but in September that year the clerk was ordered to write to the District Council, complaining of the unsatisfactory condition of the sewage works at the workhouse. The following year Mr Springall was engaged to put the drains in order, although in April 1912 local cottagers were still complaining of the bad and unhealthy smells from the workhouse drainage.

Part of the problem seems to have been created by storm water running into the existing inadequate drainage.

The Guardians frequently took over the rights and power of parents if they decided that children were at risk. In August 1910 this happened to Edith and Frederick Took, aged 11 and 7 respectively. The Guardians considered the 'habits and mode of life of Kate Took', the children's mother, to be such she was unfit to have control of the children. When another pauper, Charles Heyhoe, was sentenced to imprisonment in November 1911 for an offence against one of his children, the Guardians took the children, Blanch aged 12, Ivy aged 9 and William aged 9, into the workhouse and subsequently boarded them out with foster parents. Their mother was considered unfit by reason of mental deficiency and mode of life, and a later attempt to regain her children in September 1912 was unsuccessful.

On Monday 9th January 1911 the master, Robert Neville, was awoken at 2 o'clock in the morning by the porter, to be told that there was a policeman at the gate who had brought a man from Whissonsett to be placed in the workhouse. The man, a labourer, Robert Barker, aged 72, had in a fit of depression attempted to cut his throat. After he had been examined by the local doctor, the Parish Overseer considered that he could not be looked after at home and should be admitted to the workhouse and signed an admission order. Neville, who was suffering from a cold and probably not very happy at being woken up at such an early time, went downstairs to consult with the porter but did not go to the gate to see Barker. As the doctor's note on the back of the Admitting Order stated that no vessels were injured, Neville considered the case one for the police alone and refused to admit the man. Barker was taken back to Whissonsett at 4 o'clock and was recovered

The porter's door next to the main gates

enough to be seen in East Dereham the following Friday.

The Rector of Whissonsett, Rev. C. P. C. Seagrim, having been involved at the beginning of the case by getting the Overseer to write the Admission Order, wrote that day to the Local Government Board. Seagrim also visited Gressenhall the following day and found Neville to be 'most rude and aggressive'. His reception at the workhouse may not have been helped by being kept in the waiting room for three hours, where there was only one chair and a bench and a fire that was nearly out, all of which according to Seagrim resulted in him catching cold for ten days. The Local Government Board responded by sending their Inspector, Captain Hervey, to interview the Master, Porter and Policeman, but he did not speak to any of the Guardians. As a result of his report the Local Government Board wrote on 31st March that they considered 'Mr Neville was most seriously to blame in refusing to admit Robert Barker' and that they felt justified in asking for his resignation.

At the following board meeting, on 3rd April, the clerk laid before the board the letter the Local Government Board had sent to Neville requesting his resignation from the workhouse. The Guardians, although they felt that Neville had made a mistake in refusing admission, had endorsed his actions and considered themselves equally responsible. The clerk was immediately ordered to write a letter in reply asking the

Local Government Board to reconsider their decision. On 1st May the Local Government Board replied that they had 'carefully reconsidered the representations' but were not prepared to vary their decision. The Guardians decided to petition the board along with their local Members of Parliament to get the decision reversed. This seems to have had little impact as in a reply on 25th May the board felt that 'they must adhere to the decision which had already been communicated to the Guardians'. That same day Laura Neville, the matron, submitted her resignation on the grounds of ill health; obviously the uncertainty of the allegation and the stress caused by not knowing whether they had a job or not had taken its toll.

The tone of the correspondence from the Local Government Board seems to have been resented by the Guardians. They viewed with 'considerable disquietude the increasing insolence and arrogance of department officials in their dealings'. This was a view that was obviously shared by other unions in Norfolk as Gressenhall's Guardians received backing on 12th June from the Guardians of the Henstead Union. The situation was still unresolved on 26th June when the Guardians temporarily reappointed the Nevilles to carry out the duties of master and matron until the appointment of a successor. The Guardians now demanded a full public inquiry into the matter viewing with 'grave apprehension for the future the way at which they have been completely ignored by the Local Government Board in the arbitrary dismissal of their servant' – a view endorsed by boards of Guardians throughout the county. On 19th July the Local Government Board replied stating that they still did not see the need for an inquiry, and that they would not allow Robert Neville to remain the workhouse master and that the Guardians should make fresh appointments and

Robert Neville

terminate at once the arrangements whereby the Nevilles were acting as master and matron. With the continuing intransigence of the Local Government Board the Guardians were forced to cancel the Nevilles' appointments. However, they were still unhappy and a proposal was made, and agreed by 35 to 5 votes, that the appointment of a new master should be left to the Local Government Board itself, and another telegram was sent to London declining to advertise for a replacement for the Nevilles.

At the same meeting it was also proposed that Guardians decline to attend board meetings at Gressenhall to administer the Poor Law. The Chairman was reluctant to go this far but the following week 35 Guardians attended and a motion was carried by 21 votes to 13 that unless the Local Government Board furnish full details of their inquiry the Guardians should absent themselves from any future meetings. Three weeks later the Local Government Board replied expressing regret at the motion

Robert Neville, Master, with nursing and other staff. Photograph taken about 1903.

and toning down their reply in not wishing to 'disparage the authority or direct the administration of the Guardians'. This hint of an apology seems to have allowed the chairman to propose that the Guardians advertise for a new master and matron. Some of the Guardians were still not happy and insisted that the original motion should still stand; however, when it was put to the vote the Guardians seem to have realised that they were not going to get the Local Government Board to reverse their decision and voted by 14 to 2 to place an advertisement for a new master and matron in the local papers. The Guardians drew up a testimonial on behalf of the Nevilles expressing their great regret in losing their services and stating that during their period of service they had performed their duties in a highly efficient manner. A sub-committee formed to determine their superannuation allowance recommended £43 and £32 19s 4d respectively for Neville and his wife based on 20 years and 23 years service in the Poor Law. On 18th September Mr and Mrs George Storey, from the Knighton Union workhouse, were appointed master and matron at Gressenhall.

In 1912 the Local Government Board abolished the practice of paupers receiving their out relief at pay stations. For recipients in the Mitford and Launditch Union this had been the Corn Exchange in Dereham, but now the Relieving Officer paid the paupers in their own homes.

This was obviously not popular with the Relieving Officers who now had to travel around the Union. Mr Frank Laws was severely reprimanded in October 1912 for neglecting his duty in not going on the appointed day, causing old people to have to make two journeys to receive their relief.

The Poor Law Institution Order of 1913 prohibited cards, dice, letters or printed material of an obscene nature, highly combustible articles and spirituous or fermented liquor in the workhouse. Money was removed from new arrivals and placed in safe custody. Any monies, of course, could be used to defray their cost of maintenance whilst in the workhouse. All inmates on arrival at the workhouse were searched and the offending articles removed, the information being recorded in the Inmates Property Register. Suitable items would, of course, be returned to the inmate on their release from the house. However, even then the inmate could be searched on leaving.

Children in the workhouse had always been a concern of the Guardians and the Poor Law authorities. They increasingly saw boarding out as the most desirable method of reducing the number of children being accommodated in the workhouse. In mid-1913 the Local Government Board asked what steps the Guardians were taking to remove children from the workhouse and accommodate them elsewhere, either in a children's home or through boarding out with local people. In fact the Guardians had already

One of the few photographs showing inmates at Gressenhall. It is believed that the photograph was taken in June 1914 and shows the Chaplain, Rev. John Griffith Lambert. Note the lady in a wheelchair on the right; a self-propelling chair was purchased for use in the infirmary in September 1913.

started boarding out children from March 1910 when 15 children were boarded out with foster parents. These boarded out children were regularly visited by lady representatives from the local care committee or the Relieving Officers to check on their condition. In April 1914 a committee was formed to look into providing a home for the children away from the workhouse and by August the Guardians had settled on The Hollies, a building in East Dereham owned by a Mr Ernest Gray, renting it for 14 years at a cost of £35 per annum. In March 1915, Mrs Agnes Haynes was appointed foster mother at a salary of £25 together with Miss Lucy Sparrow as assistant. Most of the children at Gressenhall were transferred to the new home; however, some especially young children stayed with their mothers and others were sent back to the workhouse as a punishment. Children were also transferred to the home from the Freebridge Lynn Union workhouse at Gayton. One child from the local school in Dereham remembers that the children from the home were usually the best dressed, this being helped in June 1915 when they were all given a second pair of boots. By April 1916 the home was becoming crowded with 26 children occupying the space meant for 19. One family of six children had to be brought back to Gressenhall, which at the time also had ten babies in residence.

The outbreak of the Great War initially had little impact on life at the workhouse. Gradually, however, as the war dragged on, the Guardians began to receive more instructions from the government and the army. In February 1915 they were asked what arrangements had been made to evacuate inmates and staff in the event of an enemy landing on the east coast. The Guardians considered that there was no safer place than the workhouse; however, they did take out insurance against damage by aircraft in August 1915. This was rather fortuitous, as the following month, on 8th September, Dereham was bombed by Zeppelin L14 causing damage and casualties.

From July 1915 soldiers billeted in the local area were allowed to bathe and have their clothes stored at the workhouse. By October, the military authorities were requesting the use of part of the building for hospital purposes. The next month the Guardians allowed the disinfecting of clothing and blankets from the Notts and Derby Mounted Brigade billeted in the local area. Some time in 1917 part of the infirmary wing was taken over by the military as a camp for German prisoners of war. The exact date of their arrival has not yet been found as the minute books for the period between 1916 and 1919 are missing; however, the records do show that in September 1919 German prisoners were still being accommodated in the building. One of the female inmates from the workhouse, Mabel Bowman, managed to get past the guards from the 3rd Regiment of the South Wales Borderers to fraternise with a German prisoner. Mabel had been an inmate at Gressenhall since July 1917 where her son Ernest had been born. Twice she had been punished for stealing items, on the latter occasion receiving 14 days imprisonment for stealing a pair of boots and absconding from the workhouse. Mabel was brought back and remained at Gressenhall where her daughter Grace was born two years later. Mabel is last heard of in October 1923 when the Guardians received a request from the workhouse in Norwich for her to be transferred back to Gressenhall. By November the last of the prisoners had been repatriated and the Guardians were putting in their claim for dilapidation caused by the military use of the building, receiving £227 pounds in compensation.

The 1920s saw increasing numbers of tramps arriving at Gressenhall, the Guardians suggesting to the Ministry of Health that additional wards should be opened to accommodate them. In 1911 Norfolk had introduced the Way Ticket system for casuals or tramps. A similar system of identity cards had been proposed by the Gressenhall Guardians in January 1894; now any tramp entering the county received a Way Ticket. On this were recorded his details and the date of entering and leaving a workhouse. Tramps were not allowed back to the same workhouse for 30 days. In the first year of the system the number of casuals in the county decreased by 4,020 or 27%. The Guardians at Gressenhall would not allow tramps to be admitted on Sundays and wrote to other Unions in Norfolk to ensure that they also kept their casuals in their wards over Sunday. By 1925 the Guardians were recommending that casuals should be detained for two nights. That year the Casual Poor (Relief) Order meant that they had to carry out substantial alterations, providing separate baths and a new boiler in the casual wards. The Guardians were reluctant to do this unless other unions in Norfolk also contributed to the cost. The alterations were finally completed at a cost of £145 in September 1926.

In the later years of the decade the casuals or tramps entering the workhouse far outnumbered the resident inmates, and by 1928 the number had reached 358 a month. Most of the tramps arriving at Gressenhall came from the Norwich workhouse and were on their way to

COUNTY OF NORFOLK.

WAY TICKET.

No.

Name ....

From ....

To ....

Occupation ....

Age ....

Hair ....

Eyes ....

Height ....

Distinguishing Marks (if any) ....

Date ....

Signed ....

Master.

The Master of each Workhouse at which the above-named shall stay will please enter here the

Name of Workhouse ....

Date of Arrival ....

Date of Departure ....

Name of Workhouse ....

Date of Arrival ....

Date of Departure ....

Name of Workhouse ....

Date of Arrival ....

Date of Departure ....

Walsingham, Docking or Aylsham workhouses. For some reason the tramps tended to avoid entering Swaffham workhouse. In July 1929 a letter was received from a Mr A. J. Patterson at Bawdeswell, a local shop keeper, declining to supply bread and cheese to tramps en route from Gressenhall to Aylsham workhouse. It now fell to the Gressenhall workhouse master to supply bread and cheese to the tramps before they left. This was paid for by the County Council from September.

The early 1920s saw concerns at the level of nursing staff at Gressenhall to cope with the increasing numbers of elderly and infirm inmates. The Ministry of Health considered that the nursing staff should consist of a head nurse (usually the matron), two charge nurses and two assistants together with two to three probationer nurses. The extra nurses were received in time

as by November 1928 Gressenhall was receiving male inmates from Swaffham Workhouse as that building was being closed down. Swaffham union was required to pay either 15 shillings a week fixed charge and £130 annual charge for overheads or a fixed charge of 20 shillings a week for each inmate.

During the late 1920s the ladies of the Fakenham British Legion concert party would regularly entertain the inmates. The visitors would collect eggs in a tin bath, which were then presented to the inmates. It was said that these were the only eggs that inmates received from one year to the next. In 1934 the master was allowed to purchase some 2,000 eggs and a wine butt in which to preserve them.

Former tramps' lodgings, photographed in 1976

8 Poor Law Institution

THE LOCAL Government Act in April 1930 finally abolished boards of Guardians and placed their powers with the County Councils and County Boroughs. The idea of placing workhouses under County Councils had been looked at as far back as 1909, though at the time the Gressenhall Guardians considered they could provide a more personal interest in the care of the poor in their own area. In 1926 the Guardians again became concerned at proposals to transfer their powers to the County Council, considering the Rural District Councils to be more appropriate due to their local knowledge. Despite their concerns the new Act placed provision of relief for the poor with Public Assistance Committees at County level. Gressenhall was taken over by the County Council as a Public Assistance Institution for the elderly, sick and orphans and was now run by Guardians Committee Number 10, consisting of some 15 to 20 people many of whom were ex-Guardians. As a result of the new legislation the Guardians' clerk, Walter John Barton, was forced to resign after 23 years' service.

Although the 19th-century Poor Law was no more, the change seems to have had little impact on the day to day life of the inmates at Gressenhall. Small changes did occur such as the discontinuance of the handwritten minutes in a bound minute book and the appearance of typed sheets from July 1931. Also the term 'workhouse' disappears from the minutes, being replaced by 'Institution'; inmates were now called 'patients'.

Conditions in the new Public Assistance Institution gradually improved for the inmate patients. In January 1932 they received newspapers such as the *Daily Mirror*, *Daily Sketch*, *Daily Graphic* and *Daily Mail* – presumably *The Times* and the *Manchester Guardian* were considered above them.

During 1931 and 1932 the Guardians and perhaps the patients were keenly awaiting the connection of electricity to the building. This anticipation was somewhat tempered by the projected cost of £99 5s 4d per annum quoted by the Norwich Corporation. After investigation by the County Architect the cost was reduced to £68 9s 4d by reducing the number of lights fitted. In October 1932 the male patients were provided with tweed suits in place of the Hospital Blue suits they had worn previously, and a year later woollen coats were being provided to the old people in the infirmary.

One result of the Local Government Act was rationalisation of the workhouse system in Norfolk with a number of workhouses being closed. Gressenhall received inmates from Swaffham Union and in June 1934 from the Walsingham Institution. The increased numbers necessitated alterations to the building and to accommodate the new arrivals the master had to arrange the transfer of the remaining children in Gressenhall to the Children's Home in Dereham.

The Children's Home in East Dereham continued to operate, although in February 1925 the Guardians had written to the Ministry of Health for permission to board out all the children over three years old and to close it. This the Ministry of Health was reluctant to do and three years later the Guardians attempted to purchase a house in Church Street, Dereham for £650 as a new Children's Home. However, the purchase fell through and another property at 15 Norwich Road was obtained for £1050. By September 1929 the new home was accommodating 20 children, necessitating the employment in 1932 of a second assistant. Agnes Haynes had been foster mother at the home since it opened but in

Gressenhall Poor Assistance Institution about 1932. Left to right: Back row: 1 ?, 2 Nurse Chaplin, 3 J. Larwood (Relieving Officer), 4 Nurse ?, 5 Babbage (Relieving Officer), 6 Nurse Ivy Sparrow (later Mrs W. Carr), 7 Nurse Eileen Olive Woods (later Mrs Dorman), 8 Nurse Doris M. Grimes, 9 Miss E. M. Norman (Nursery Nurse), 10 Sister Ida Daisy Arnell, 11 Mr Yull (office staff), 12 Nurse Irene Long, 13 Mr Wright (office staff). Front row: 1 Nurse Edith Mary Hewson, 2 Porter, 3 Mrs Duigan, 4 Mr Reginald Guy (Master), 5 Mrs Guy (Matron), 6 Dr Duigan, 7 Cook, Porter's Wife, 8 H. Barker (Engineer). In front: 1 Peter Ransome Guy (Master's son, born 1924), 2 Porter's son.

later years she had increasing difficulty in maintaining discipline in the home and when one of the girls, Mildred Maud, a frequent absconder, broke property, it final led to Agnes retiring in July 1947. The Guardians were to have difficulty in finding a replacement for Agnes and to ease the situation they restricted the age of the boys in the home to under 11.

Continual improvements and expansion of facilities for tramps were made in the early 1930s. Additional bathing facilities and extra rooms for up to 50 more casuals were converted. A shed was erected in the yard in which they carried out sawing and chopping of wood. An extra 2½ acres of land was brought back from the Union Farm tenant, Richard Ayres, in 1933 to provide work for the casuals in the planting and raising of potatoes. Throughout the 1930s large numbers of casuals passed through Gressenhall, sometimes averaging 400 to 500 a month. In the early years of the Second World War, the main casual wards in the county, including Gressenhall, were closed. This may have been done to reduce movement in the East Anglian area, although it is to be wondered what happened to all the tramps.

The Guardians' Committee were saddened in December 1931 by the loss of their chairman, Alfred George Copeman. Copeman had been a member of the Board of Guardians for many years, the last 32 as chairman, and was described as 'one of the few men who spend their

Hannah Brunton, an inmate of Beech House who helped with the children; she was a resident 'on the house side'; the photograph was taken about 1935/6 in the infants' yard.

lives in doing work for which they received no payment.' He was succeeded by George Brett, another long-serving Guardian – he began in 1899 and remained in post until he died in February 1942.

Friction amongst the staff surfaced in February 1933 when six nurses in the workhouse infirmary complained to the House Committee about the changes the matron, Mrs Robinson, was making to their duty schedules. The Robinsons seem to have had a number of complaints made against them and the Guardians voted by 16 votes to 0 to terminate their employment, considering them 'unsuitable officers'. The Public Assistance Committee sent a sub-committee to Gressenhall to investigate but found that there was insufficient evidence to warrant the Robinsons' appointments to be terminated. They did though find that the Robinsons had not been tactful in their dealings with the staff and the Guardians and did not work harmoniously with the Guardians' Committee. Their recommendation was that the pair should look for another post in the interest of themselves and the Institution. The Robinsons obviously mended their ways as they did not finally retire from Gressenhall until 1935.

Another master and matron, Mr and Mrs Loxham, also seem to have caused friction amongst the staff and inmates. In July 1938 trouble arose

Staff in 1935: in the front row are the Master, James Robinson, and his wife Jane, the Matron.

Board room of Gressenhall Union Workhouse, showing the retirement party in 1935 of Master and Matron James Edward & Jane Robinson (standing behind chair at back). To the left of them in grey jacket/white shirt is the Labour Master, believed to be Herbert A. W. Musto; next to the Vicar, Charlie Scace (Porter); 7th from front on right Mrs Thompson (then Miss Wicks), Nursing attendant.

between the matron and the cook over provision of meals for the nurses. The master, Mr Loxton, promptly suspended the cook but was informed that he had no authority to do so. That same day he was also criticised for using physical violence to control an epileptic inmate, William Dovers, who had been falsely accused of taking items from a room he was supposed to be cleaning. The following month the Public Assistance Committee found the Loxhams 'totally unfitted to be in charge of the Gressenhall Institution', and recommended their resignation.

The sort of situations in which workhouse officers could find themselves is revealed by an incident in March 1934. The porter, Mr Whitehead, was called before the Guardians and severely reprimanded and cautioned as to his conduct, having assaulted a patient, Thomas Wright, blackening his eye and bruising his face, albeit under great provocation.

The outbreak of war in September 1939 seems initially to have had little impact of life at the workhouse. Gradually however, Gressenhall began to receive evacuees from other institutions, 68 patients arriving temporarily from the Pulham Market Institution in August 1940 as well as patients from Rochford Institution in Essex the following year. In September 1940 work was started in carrying out alterations to the cellar for use as an air raid shelter. This was opportune as a reference in the minutes of November 1940 refers to the repair of damage as result of enemy action, suggesting the building had been bombed. The damage may have been caused by an enemy bombing raid on the nearby Royal Air Force station at Swanton Morley which was bombed on 5th November. Cost of repair was only £2 8s 0d so the damage must have been slight.

Patients who were paid for work done in the workhouse were from October 1933 regarded as Petty Officers of the County Council. In December 1941 the Guardians asked for a number of patients to be paid for the useful work they had carried out. William Grant, 63, helped in the casual wards bathing tramps, and also drove the pony and trap to Dereham once a day. Edward Platter, 67, was employed painting the building and cleaning drains and lavatories, while Frances Grace, 50, attended to the heating boilers.

On the night of 23rd January 1942 a fire started in one of the nurses' rooms in the south-east corner of the building. Discovered by the local policeman, Constable E. Worby, it soon gained a hold and 60 patients in the east wing had to be evacuated. Constable Worby stayed all night working alongside the staff, valiantly fighting the fire with stirrup pumps under the direction of the master, D. J. Nichols, and helping in the evacuation of the inmates. The fire services took an hour to arrive, the Norwich brigade arriving some ten minutes before the one from Dereham. The damage to the building was mainly in three nurses' bedrooms and was repaired by July. As a result of the fire the master and matron were awarded payment for clothing destroyed, while Nurse Waller, in whose room the fire was believed to have started, had to wait until June for her repayment as there was some disagreement as to the amount being claimed. The Guardians investigated the possibility of a complaint against the fire services but in the end decided that due to the uncertainty of the time when they were called, no useful purpose would be served. However over the following weeks rumours circulated throughout the neighbourhood which the Dereham fire brigade were keen to quash. There was concern at the time that the fire would have acted as a beacon for German bombers. It was only three months later that Norwich suffered heavy bombing raids, badly damaging the Norwich Poor Assistance Institution at Bowthorpe, from which 28 patients were transferred to Gressenhall.

The master normally recorded the movement of patients in and out of the Institution in his report book, but in November 1943 the minutes recorded that a pig had been transferred to Aylsham Institution. By the 1940s the Industrial Farm, set up in 1851 to teach the children agricultural skills, was mainly concerned with the rearing of pigs. 'Digging for Victory' meant that the land around the building was all ploughed up and potatoes planted.

In May 1944 allegations were made against the officers and management at Gressenhall concerning the question of the condition of some children from the Norwell family who had recently been discharged. The Guardians were so concerned at this smear on their reputation that they immediately requested the Public Assistance Committee to undertake proceedings for libel against the complainant. The Public Assistance Committee replied that they could not take proceedings for libel on behalf of staff but felt that 'no harm had been done to the officers as the committee's confidence in them had not been shaken'.

KEEPING NEAR THE RELATIVES

Gressenhall's Guardians would often transfer patients to other workhouses to allow them to be nearer relatives and friends. Not all Unions were so obliging; William Barber, 82, for instance, was removed from Aylsham district in November 1946 to Gressenhall. The Guardians strongly protested against 'the removal of old people away from their homes making it impossible for them to be visited by their friends and relatives'.

With the end of the war most of the workhouses in Norfolk changed their names, removing any reference to being an Institution. In October Gressenhall's Guardians' Committee recommended that the name of the building should be changed to 'Beech House'. The name 'Beech House' or 'Beech Hill' had first been used in 1919 when the Registrar General's Office deleted references to Poor Law Institutions on death certificates. The end of the war also saw improvements making life better for the patients and staff and attempts to lose the 'workhouse feel' of the building. The windows in the infirmary wards were lowered by two feet to allow patients in bed to see out, and light coloured paint was used to decorate rooms. Rooms were converted for recreation and entertainment areas for staff and patients. The labour master and laundress living in what is now Cherry Tree Cottage must have been very grateful for a bath being installed in the cottage. Prior to this they had been forced to use the bath in the casuals' ward.

At long last in January 1947 the forms on which the inmates had sat to eat their meals in the dining room were replaced by chairs. The long tables were however retained, and an example survives today in the museum. By 1947 the population of Gressenhall increasingly consisted of elderly people, a factor which led to the workhouse becoming a County home for the elderly when the Poor Law system and workhouses were finally abolished in 1948.

9 Old People's Home to Museum

THE NATIONAL Assistance Act in 1948 finally abolished the Poor Law; relief was now to be provided by the National Assistance Board. The austere forbidding workhouses were now converted to county homes for the elderly, hospitals or offices. Gressenhall was converted to an old people's home with Iris Smith being appointed the first matron. She had actually arrived as the assistant matron but was promoted in a matter of a few weeks when the original matron left. Many of the patients were of course already well established, having been patients in the old workhouse.

After the Second World War parts of Gressenhall, mainly the buildings along the west side of the site, became a half-way house for displaced families. Many of these were women with large families. They were not happy to be there, they felt it was demeaning that they were forced to obtain their food from the main hall the same as the pauper residents of the workhouse. Many remember their time at Gressenhall with disgust and shame at being placed in the workhouse by the local council. Social Services dealt with these families, but as their offices were not open over the weekend any problems had usually to be dealt with by the superintendent and matron of Beech House.

The council continued to use the building for housing evicted and homeless families after it became an old people's home. In 1958 the local paper was refused permission to inspect the area these families were living in, although they were allowed to inspect the rest of the main building. The site was still being used as casual accommodation for vagrants who were given a night's lodging for an hour's work.

The nurses at Beech House wore a blue and white striped dress with white aprons, stiff collar and black lisle stockings. Women residents were issued with a navy blue serge dress and a cross-over apron whilst the men were issued with a navy serge suit. All the clothing had name tags sown on showing that it came from Beech House.

In the late 1950s and early 1960s the home was run by Mr and Mrs G. E. Gerald, as superintendent and matron. The Geralds maintained a free and easy atmosphere, there was little or no regimentation, and none of the patients were obliged to work. There were a number of lounges, all with radio, and as in many other institutions a television was temporarily placed in the main hall to allow the residents to watch the coronation of Queen Elizabeth II in 1953. The dining hall was used for entertainment with a stage erected at the west end. Residents received 10 shillings a week pocket money, free tobacco, cigarettes and sweets, and if their own clothes were unwearable they were given new ones. The Geralds had the rooms painted in gay colours and attempted to split up the dormitories into smaller homely sleeping quarters. The latter had been of some concern to correspondents in the local papers in 1959, who objected to residents still being accommodated in dormitories. In reply Ethel Tipple, chairman of the Norfolk Welfare Committee, said that the design of the building made it difficult to provide single rooms and that many residents preferred the companionship and security of the dormitory.

Gressenhall at this time was the recipient of much help from American servicemen from nearby RAF Sculthorpe. In 1958 airmen from the base had installed the electric lighting in the chapel. Two Americans in particular, Master Sergeant Paul Stenba and his wife Lindy, were regular visitors to the home. Mrs Stenba first came to Gressenhall with a Girl Guide group to sing carols and 'fell in love' with the home. In 1961 on returning to the States she said how much 'my lovely old people' had made their tour of duty in England 'truly wonderful'.

The Geralds were leading lights in the East Dereham Rotary Club, Mr Gerald becoming President in 1962 whilst Mrs Gerald was Vice President of the Inner Wheel. Both were active members of the St John Ambulance Brigade as was the home's doctor, E. J. Puddy. In June 1963 Gressenhall was visited by the then Minister of Health, Enoch Powell. At the time 144 elderly people were resident in the home.

There was further correspondence in the local

Men's dining room, 1975

Women's dormitory in 1975

Residents in their day room, 1974   *East wing upper corridor, 1974*

papers in 1963 as to the standard of accommodation in the house. Rooms were supposed to be devoid of carpets and in rows of chairs sat old ladies on a bare floor. In reply one resident said that when she had first arrived at Gressenhall the bathroom had been cold and open, but now it was private and warm and that whilst a few years ago there were just hard chairs or forms to sit on and no curtains at the windows this had all been changed during the time of the Geralds. After nine years' service the Geralds left in 1966, Mr Gerald becoming a priest in the Church of England.

By the 1970s the use of old workhouse buildings for accommodating elderly people was no longer acceptable and gradually they were closed down and the residents transferred to new homes. Gressenhall was the last of Nor-folk's workhouses to be retained as an old people's home. In June 1974 some 45 residents were transferred to a new residential home for the elderly at Glaven Hale in Holt. Mrs Iris Smith and her husband became the managers of the new home having been the matron and superintendent at Gressenhall. Many had lived at Gressenhall for over 20 years and the move was quite traumatic, not least in that they were now accommodated in single rooms whereas before they had been in dormitories of 12 or more. It was noted that the new residents tended to leave their doors open to recreate the dormitory feel. Many of these residents also suffered from anti-social and mental health problems.

The last superintendent and matron at Gressenhall were Wendy and Morris Lyons, who arrived in April 1973, starting off as deputy superintendent and matron but soon taking over as superintendent and matron in June 1974, when the Smiths left for Glaven Hale. Wendy Lyons was a night sister with full nursing qualifications whilst Morris was an ex-engineer who took a course to gain qualifications. As deputies they were lodged in Cherry Tree Cottages and on promotion moved to the old master's wing, their children's board and lodging having to be paid for just as was the case when the building was a workhouse.

Staff at the home consisted of one couple as superintendent and matron, one couple as deputy superintendent and matron, six male carers for the elderly men, women carers for the elderly women, one full-time painter and decorator, one maintenance man who lived in, two gardeners who supplied the home with vegetables and looked after the gardens and tennis courts, two seamstresses sewing old and second-hand clothes and staff in the laundry and kitchens.

In 1972 there were 130 residents who came from all over Norfolk including Yarmouth and King's Lynn and not just Mitford and Launditch. The men lived in the north and the women in the south of the building. There were several day rooms for the residents where they could meet and plenty of space if they wanted to get away from each other. They could bring in

Residents in the kitchen of Beech House, 1974.

valuables with them which could be kept under lock and key of the superintendent or matron if they wished. There was a tuck shop on site where the residents could purchase little luxuries like cigarettes, sweets or toiletries and fruit. A little pocket money could be earned by doing jobs around the home of a light nature if they wished. Profits from the shop went to the Amenities Fund. The residents were allowed a bit of pocket money from their pension but those who smoked had a problem managing. One resident of the home was an expert mole catcher and his skills were much in demand in the local area and several people would go to the home asking for the services of 'Moley'!

The old men were allowed out to the local public houses with permission. They would walk under their own steam and after a drink would get the landlord to contact the Gressenhall staff who had to go and collect them. On one occasion an old gentleman who regularly went into Norwich on a Saturday to visit his son got into difficulties and unfortunately died in Golden Ball Street in Norwich. He had little identification on him except that his clothes had Beech House written on them so that they were able to track him down to Gressenhall.

Overnight there were two staff on duty and there was also a sick ward. The staff would check the dormitories in the mornings to see if all the residents were all right. Some elected to stay in bed and were allowed to. By June 1974 there were 68 residents as half had moved out to Fakenham.

There was a church service at 9.30 in the chapel and David Brough the organist from Beetley Methodist church played the organ with the service taken by Rev. Mr Wilks from Gressenhall church. On Sunday there was a Christian Fellowship Service in the afternoon led by the Congregational minister, Rev. Ken Banks. The Free Church Council was involved in services. On Friday evenings there were whist drives.

By 28th January 1975 the remaining residents were transferred to new homes, the elderly women going to Huntingfields at Costessey. By 30th January the men had also all left, except one old gentleman who sat on the staircase and flatly refused to go to 'foreign parts'; eventually he was found a place at Fakenham.

The building did not stay empty for long. During 1974 local government was reorganised in England and one of the effects was the formation of the Norfolk Museums Service. Prior to this, town museums were situated in Norwich, Thetford, Kings Lynn and Yarmouth but there was no museum to tell the story of the county as a whole. Bridget Yates, a curator from the Norwich Museums, was sent to tour the county to find a suitable location. Having briefly looked at a number of other buildings in the county, including the workhouse at Wicklewood, the decision was made to use Gressenhall and plans were drawn up to convert Beech House into the Norfolk Rural Life Museum. A report to the County's Museum Committee in July 1974 recommended the conversion despite some opposition that there was already a rural life museum at Stowmarket in Suffolk, with concern being expressed that there was not a need for two museums from adjacent counties trying to show rural life in what was the unified area of East Anglia; however, by November the committee had given approval.

A Friends organisation was formed in 1975 after a meeting at Anglia House in Norwich, chaired by TV presenter Dick Joice. The Friends set out to support the new museum by fundraising and soon had 230 members. In September 1975 the Friends organised an open day at which 3,000 attended.

Bridget Yates was appointed full-time curator in April 1976 and initially only had one helper and two maintenance men from the County Council, although there was a great deal of support from the Friends. A five-year development plan was drafted with a capital input of £50,000 per year being proposed. The first few years were spent in building up the collection and repairing the building. Through the generosity of Norfolk people the first simple displays were opened in 1976. Much of the early work was done by apprentices from Eastern Electricity who helped to restore a number of steam engines for display.

By August 1976 the need for more display and

This building, formerly used as tramps' lodgings, became the Museum's first tea-room.

storage space had become apparent and approval was given by the Museums Committee to enclose the north courtyard necessitating the demolition of the boiler house and chimney. The application was finally approved by Breckland Council and work started in February 1979. The money for the conversion, some £40,000, was raised by the Friends under the able chairmanship of Dick Joice.

In 1977 the local Women's Institute committee held a competition to design an interior for Cherry Tree Cottage under the title 'The Way They/We Lived Then'. Seven clubs produced models of the rooms, the winners being a tie between the North/South Wootton and Hellesdon Women's Institutes. The cottage was finally opened to the public in May 1981.

The Norfolk Rural Life Museum was officially

opened by the Hon Robin Walpole MP on 19th July 1977 and during the first week over 1,000 people visited. During the early years the museum opened for the summer season between May and September with a least one 'major' event being organised by the Friends.

Union Farm had continued in operation as a tenanted farm but in September 1979 the last tenant, Fred Duffield, retired. The farm was handed over to the Friends on a three-year lease with Fred staying on in the farmhouse to help the Friends develop the farm as a 19th-century farm with rare breeds and traditional working. One of the reasons for selection of Gressenhall as the Rural Life Museum had been the availability of the farm. By 1987, however, the future of the farm was in some doubt with the Friends having difficulty in raising the £30,000 running expenses. By 1989 the decision was made for the museum to take over the running of the farm officially and a farm manager, Richard Dalton, was appointed to help integrate the farm into the museum complex.

In 1994 Bridget Yates finally retired from Gressenhall to take up a new post as Director of Communications for the Norfolk Museums Service and a new curator, Andrew Mackay, was appointed.

During the early years of the museum little was made of the original history of the building as a workhouse; the burial ground was planted as an orchard in 1995 housing many varieties of old Norfolk apples. However in March 1998 a major exhibition 'Life and Death in the Workhouse' was opened, sponsored by Anglia Funeral Services.

In 1999 work started on a major refurbishment programme for the museum. Funded through grants from the Heritage Lottery Fund, European regional funds, the East of England Development Agency and the Friends of Gressenhall, the major part of the work consisted of strengthening the first floor ceiling to allow the upstairs rooms to be used for display, offices and storage. At the same time the display in the building underwent a major upgrade. The Museum reopened in July 2000 after a delay due to the outbreak of foot and mouth in the country.

Today Gressenhall Farm and Workhouse form a major tourist attraction in the county showing visitors how life was lived in the country years ago; large numbers of school children come on educational visits. The story of the building's early days as House of Industry and Union workhouse is now shown in a series of rooms along the east corridor and future plans are being drafted to open more of the building to the visitor, including the laundry.

It is difficult now to imagine life in the workhouse amongst the chatter and laughter of exited children visiting the museum. However the displays and information on show at Gressenhall do remember the Poor Law and its effect on the lives of those unfortunates forced to enter its walls. It is a curious paradox of the workhouse that although life for an inmate was hard, materially they could be better off inside, where they had a roof over their head, regular if monotonous food and their children received an education. However, the psychological effect of having to ask for relief and being forced to enter the workhouse meant that they were always considered bad places. Many workhouses fulfilled a useful function as a place of last resort for many disadvantaged people. The museum is continuing to research the inmates and staff of the workhouse so that their lives will not be forgotten.

The House of Industry at Gressenhall, depicted in an oil painting by Robert Kerrison, 1810. The painting (which was purchased from Prince Duleep Singh in 1926) is displayed at Gressenhall, on loan from Thetford Museum.

Plan 1

The Buildings in 1780

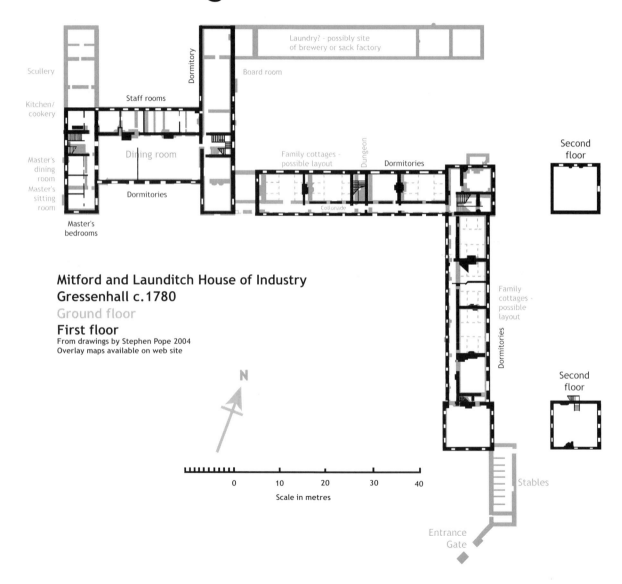

Scullery

Kitchen/ cookery

Staff rooms

Dormitory

Board room

Laundry? - possibly site of brewery or sack factory

Dining room

Master's dining room

Master's sitting room

Dormitories

Master's bedrooms

Family cottages - possible layout

Dungeon

Dormitories

Collonade

Second floor

Family cottages - possible layout

Dormitories

Second floor

Mitford and Launditch House of Industry
Gressenhall c.1780
Ground floor
First floor
From drawings by Stephen Pope 2004
Overlay maps available on web site

N

Stables

0 10 20 30 40

Scale in metres

Entrance Gate

Plan 2
The Buildings in 1930

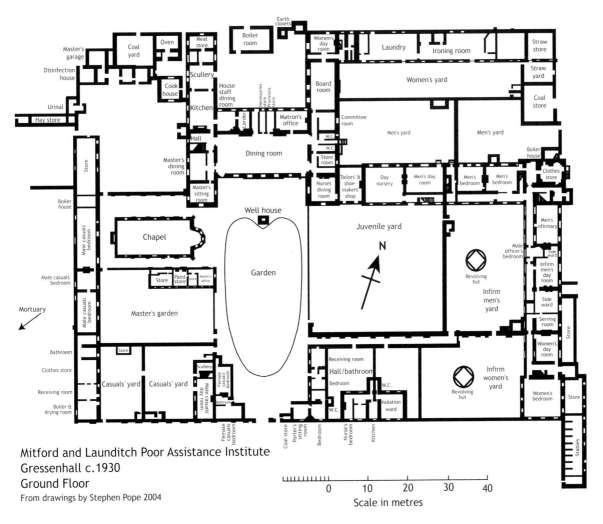

Master's garage · Coal yard · Oven · Meat store · Boiler room · Earth closets · Women's day room · Laundry · Ironing room · Straw store · Straw yard · Disinfection house · Scullery · House staff dining room · Necessaries store · Provisions store · Board room · Women's yard · Coal store · Cook house · Kitchen · Larder · Matron's office · Committee room · Urinal · Hay store · Hall · W.C. · W.C. · Men's yard · Men's yard · Boiler house · Master's dining room · Dining room · Store room · Clothes store · Master's sitting room · Nurses dining room · Tailors' & shoe-makers' shop · Day nursery · Men's day room · Men's bedroom · Men's bedroom · Store · Well house · Men's infirmary · Boiler house · Chapel · Garden · Juvenile yard · Revolving hut · Male officer's bedroom · Side ward · Infirm men's day room · Male casuals' bedroom · Store · Paint store · Store · Master's office · N · Side ward · Male casuals' bedroom · Mortuary · Master's garden · Infirm men's yard · Serving room · Bathroom · Store · Women's day room · Store · Clothes store · Scullery · Receiving room · Revolving hut · Casuals' yard · Casuals' yard · Female casuals' bedroom · Male casuals' day room · Hall/bathroom · Bedroom · W.C. · Infirm women's yard · Women's bedroom · Store · Receiving room · Bathroom · Isolation ward · Boiler & drying room · W.C. · Stables · Female casuals' bedroom · Coal store · Porter's sitting room · Bedroom · Nurse's bedroom · Kitchen

Mitford and Launditch Poor Assistance Institute
Gressenhall c.1930
Ground Floor
From drawings by Stephen Pope 2004

0   10   20   30   40
Scale in metres

Appendix 1
Mitford & Launditch Union Parishes

Eynesford Hundred

Bawdeswell
Billingford
Bintry
Bylaugh
Elsing
Foxley
Guist
Lyng
Sparham
Twyford

Launditch Hundred

Beetley
Brisley
Colkirk
East Bilney
East Lexham
Gateley
Great Dunham
Great Fransham
Gressenhall
Hoe
Horningtoft
Kempstone
Litcham
Little Dunham
Little Fransham
Longham
Mileham
Beeston All Saints with Bittering
North Elmham
Oxwick & Pattesley
Rougham
Scarning
Stanfield
Swanton Morley
Tittleshall
Weasenham St Peter
Weasenham All Saints
Wellingham
Wendling
West Lexham
Whissonsett
Worthing

Mitford Hundred

Cranworth
East Dereham
East Tuddenham
Garveston
Hardingham
Hockering
Letton
Mattishall
Mattishall Burgh
North Tuddenham
Reymerston
Shipdham
South Burgh
Thuxton
Westfield
Winburgh
Wood Rising
Yaxham

Appendix 2
Gressenhall Workhouse Staff and Union Officials

The date at the left is the date of arrival, the date at the right is the date of departure; dates in italics are the first or last recorded mention of the person but may not be the actual date they arrived or left. These lists are also available on the publisher's website, www.poppyland.co.uk in the 'Support and Resources' section, where they are supplemented by lists of all inmates, and of assistants to the matron, barbers, cleaners, clerical staff, cooks, engineers, handymen, labour masters, laundry staff, medical officers, messengers, nurses, organists, painters, porters, pupil teachers, seamstresses, servants, shoemakers, tailors and other assistants, and of union officials such as committee chairmen; it is possible to conduct a computer search for any name.

CHAIRMAN OF GUARDIANS

1836	Frederick Walpole Keppel	1842
1842	Rev. Thomas Padden	1849
1849	Frederick Walpole Keppel	1852
1852	Rev. Philip Gurdon (*Shipdham*)	*1864*
1867	Richard Charles Browne Esq.	1893
	Resigned through ill health; died April 1893	
1893	Thomas Henry Hubbard (*North Elmham*)	1899
1899	Alfred George Copeman	*1934*
	Little Dunham Lodge, Swaffham	
1915	J. P. Hudson	*1915*
1933	George Brett JP CA	1942
	East Dereham; died 1942	
1939	Harry W. Fox	*1946*

MASTER

1777	James Moore	
	First Master, formerly innkeeper of the George Hotel, East Dereham	
1836	Edward Tice	1837
1837	George Pinson	1843
	Children: Harriot, Charlotte, Henry, George	
1843	George Francis Whelan	1846
1846	Stephen Wade	1850
	Resigned through wife's ill health	
1850	Henry Harrison	1858
	Child: Elizabeth	
1858	Robert William Scraggs	1868
	Resigned through ill health	
1868	Philip John Reynolds	1897
	Former Relieving Officer Litcham District	
	Children: Fanny, Charles	
1897	Charles Henry Knight	1898
	Served for 8 months	

1898 James Thomas Tanner 1899
1899 Robert Neville 1911
Forced to resign by Local Government Board
1911 George Storey 1914
1914 Harold Burton Holmes (*of Pickering*) 1918
1918 R. P. Perkins 1924
1924 Reginald H. Guy 1932
1932 James Edward Robinson *retired* 1935
1936 C. Farnsworth
— Loxham *dismissed* 1938
1938 D. J. Nichols 1946
1946 A. E. White (*formerly at West Beckham*)

MATRON

1777 Margaret Moore 1781
Buried in Dereham churchyard
1782 Elizabeth Moore 1782
Died 3 March 1782. Buried in Dereham
1836 Martha Tice 1837
1837 Rhoda Pinson 1843
1843 Emma Whelan 1846
1846 Sophia Wade *resigned through ill health* 1850
1850 Margaret Harrison 1858
1858 Mary Ann Scraggs 1868
Died aged 58. Buried in Dereham
1868 Beloy Ann Lucy Reynolds 1896
1897 Miriam Knight 1897
Served for 4 months
1898 Georgina Tanner 1899
1899 Mrs Laura S. Neville *resigned through ill health* 1911
1911 Mary Ellen Storey 1914
1914 Mrs Holmes 1918

1918 M. M. Perkins 1924
Appointed head nurse of infirmary in 1921
1924 Mrs R. R. Guy 1932
1932 Mrs Jane Robinson *retired* 1936
1936 Mrs Farnsworth
Mrs Loxham *dismissed* 1938
1938 Mrs M. Nichols 1946
1946 Mrs C. M. White

SCHOOLMASTER

1836 Robert Rudd *dismissed* 1838
1838 John Gibson 1840
1840 Robert Bradfield *resigned* 1874
1874 William Stinson (*Assistant*)
1874 Francis Baskham Gale 1876
ex Wantage Union – to Beetley School
1876 Frank Roach 1879
1879 Charles William Eastoe *resigned 1881*

SCHOOLMISTRESS

1836 Mary Rudd 1838
Dismissed for general misconduct
1838 Harriott Pinson
Master's daughter
1844 Ann Youngs *discharged* 1844
1844 Eliza Underwood 1845
1845 Emily Ward 1847
1847 Mary Wardlow 1847
Only there for 2 months
1847 Charlotte Sparrow (*became Charlotte Raph*) 1848

1848 Clarissa Lang
    Taught infants

1848 Miss Anna Cooper   1849

1849 Mrs Spurrell
    Taught infants

1849 Charlotte Wigg   *resigned* 1859
    Late of Saffron Walden Union

1850 Harriet Perfect   1859
    Taught infants

1859 Sarah Hambling   1859

1859 Sarah Ormiston   1867
    From South Lynn

1861 Anna Green   *resigned* 1861
    Taught infants

1861 Emma Elizabeth Carter   1861
    From the infants' school at Litcham
    Resigned through ill health

1865 Miss Agnes Cary   *1868*
    Taught infants

1867 Eliza Parry   1869

1869 Miss Mary Drake   1874

1869 Mary Ann Murrell   1870
    Taught infants. Became assistant matron

1870 Thurza Mary Miles   1871
    Taught infants

1874 Elizabeth Martha Skinner   1879

1879 Fanny Reynolds   1881
    Master's daughter

1881 Mary Ann Taylor   *resigned* 1882
    Formerly teacher at Dereham

1882 Miss Jane Battison   1882
    Served for five months

1882 Miss Mary A. Horne *(temporary)*   1882

1882 Miss Mary H. Axe   1882
    Served for one month

1882 Miss Lucy Jane Mackey   1883
    Served for five months

1883 Miss Elizabeth Haythorpe *given notice to quit* 1884

1884 *Children taught in local schools*   *1887*

1887 Miss Elizabeth Laister   1891

1888 Miss Mary Ann Stephenson   1890
    Taught infants. Served for four months

1890 Mary Barnes   1894
    Taught infants
    Married Henry Peachment, porter

1891 Miss Caroline Butler   1893
    From Pulham workhouse

1894 Minnie E. Lewis   1896
    Taught infants

1896 Miss Florence E. Chinery   1896
    Served for one month

1896 Miss E. Rivers   1898

1896 Miss Lilian M. Melton   1899
    Taught infants
    Became caretaker general assistant

Appendix 3

Acts of Parliament and Poor Law Commission General Orders

Date	Title/No	Content
1597	Poor law (9 Eliz. c3)	Parish responsible for poor
1601	Poor Law (43 Eliz. c2)	Authorities to provide relief and work Parish basic unit of administration Compulsory poor rate
1662	Act of Settlement (13&14 Ch II c12)	Gave power to Overseers to remove any newcomers to their parish of settlement
1697	(8 & 9 Wm III)	'An Act for supplying some defects in the laws for the relief of the poor of this Kingdom' Widening of parish responsibility for labourers seeking work
1772	Workhouse Test Act (9 Geo I c7) 'Knatchbull's Act'	'An Act for the Amendment of the laws relating to settlement, employment and relief of the poor' Parishes given powers to establish workhouses. Able to refuse relief to paupers who would not enter
1775	(15 Geo III c59)	'An Act for the better relief and employment of the poor within the Hundreds of Mitford and Launditch in the County of Norfolk'
1782	Gilbert's Act (22 Geo III c83)	Provided for unions of parishes to set up common workhouses Workhouses became poorhouses to aged and infirm

1795	(35 Geo III c101)	'An Act to prevent the removal of poor persons until they shall become actually chargeable' No pauper to be returned to parish of settlement until they become chargeable to poor rates of parish Removal of sick paupers suspended until recovered
1796	(36 Geo III c23) 'Sir William Young' Act	Justices could distribute relief even if applicant refused to enter workhouse
1819	(59 Geo III c12) 'Sturges Bourne's Act'	'An Act to amend the laws for the relief of the poor' Adoption of select vestries to control poor relief Salaried assistant overseers
1824	Vagrancy Act	Prohibited sleeping in open and begging in street, punishable by fortnight's hard labour
1834	Poor Law Amendment Act (4 & 5 Will IV c76)	'An Act for the amendment and better administration of the laws relating to the poor in England and Wales' National system of poor law administration Powers to group parishes into unions
1842	Outdoor Labour Test Order	Able-bodied men not to receive relief unless performing a task of work set by Guardians
1844	Outdoor Relief Prohibition Order	Relief to be given to able-bodied men, women and families only in the workhouse
1844	Poor Law Act (7 & 8 Vic c101)	Unmarried mothers able to sue putative fathers Smaller unions to combine to finance, run district schools for pauper children
1847	(10 & 11 Vic c110) 'Bodkins Act'	Whole cost of relieving poor on common fund of Union

1852	Outdoor Relief Regulation Order	Prohibited relief to able-bodied men while employed for wages
1861	Irremovability Act	Rateable value of property to be basis of parish contribution, rather than amount of expended on relief
1864	Homeless Poor Act	Central finance for Metropolitan casual wards led to improvements
1865	Union Chargeability Act (28 & 29 Vic c79)	Whole cost of relief on Union rather than parish
1867	Metropolitan Poor Act (30 & 31 Vic c6)	Central authority powers to order separate asylums for care of sick, insane or infirm in London
1870	Education Act	Children could attend Board Schools
1871	Pauper Inmates Discharge and Regulation Act (34 & 35 Vic c108)	Gave Guardians greater powers to detain inmates in workhouse and to detain casuals until they had performed a morning's work
1875	Agricultural Children's Act	Attendance of children at school
1885	Medical Relief Disqualification Removal Act (48 & 49 Vic c46)	Eliminated stigma of poor law from medical treatment Receipt of medical aid not to lead to loss of the vote
1896	Poor Law Officers Superannuation Act	Guardians compelled to contribute superannuation payments based on officers' length of service
1899	Poor Law Act	Guardians empowered to remove children from unsuitable parents
1905	Unemployed Workmen's Act (5 Ed VII c18)	Municipal distress committees established. Local authorities given power to set up Labour Exchanges and assist emigration of unemployed

1908	Old Age Pensions Act (8 Ed VII c40)	Applied to over 70 with income less than £31 10s per annum
1926	Board of Guardians (Default) Act (16 & 17 Geo V c20)	Ministry of Health empowered to dismiss elected boards of boards of Guardians
1929	Local Government Act (19 Geo V c17)	Boards of Guardians abolished, powers transferred to town and county councils
1930	Poor Law Act	Only aged and infirm could apply for workhouse care; outdoor relief to be given to all other poor
1931	Public Assistance (Casual Poor) Order	More comforts to casual wards End to stone breaking Disappearance of gruel
1946	National Health Service Act (9 & 10 Geo VI c81)	Final abolition of Poor Law and workhouses The Act came into force in 1948

Further Reading

M. A. Crowther, *The Workhouse System 1834–1929* (London: Methuen, 1983)

Anne Digby, *Pauper Palaces* (Studies in Economic History series) (London: Routledge & Kegan Paul, 1978). Deals specifically with the workhouses of Norfolk.

David Englander, *Poverty and Poor Law Reform in Britain from Chadwick to Booth, 1834–1914* (London: Longman, 1998)

Norman Longmate, *The Workhouse* (London: Maurice Temple Smith, 1974; new edition London: Pimlico, 2003). Standard work on the social history of the institution.

Trevor May, *The Victorian Workhouse* (Princes Risborough: Shire, 1997). Illustrated 32-page introduction.

Kathryn Morrison, *The Workhouse: a Study of Poor-Law Buildings in England* (Swindon: Royal Commission on Historical Monuments of England, 1999)

The Poor Law in Norfolk 1700–1850: a Collection of Source Materials edited by Jerry Crowley and Andy Reid (Ely: EARO, 1983)

Andy Reid, *The Union Workhouse: a Study Guide for Teachers and Local Historians* (Learning Local History series, 3) (Chichester: Phillimore for the British Association for Local History, 1994)

Michael E. Rose, *The English Poor Law 1780–1930* (Sources for Social and Economic History series) (Newton Abbot: David & Charles, 1971)

Websites

http://www.workhouses.org.uk is a website compiled by Peter Higginbotham covering hundreds of workhouses, including of course Gressenhall. Also gives full text of relevant national legislation and a list of useful books with links to on-line bookshops from which they may be purchased.

http://www.poppyland.co.uk is the website for the publisher of the present book. Its Support and Resources section includes much additional information on the staff of Gressenhall (see page 97 above). A range of titles on Norfolk and Suffolk history is also available from the site.

Index

Excluding the Appendixes – to hunt for names in lists, use the web version at www.poppyland.co.uk